AUTISM

AND

EMPLOYMENT

Raising Your Child With Foundational Skills For The Future

D1406912

Lisa Tew, MS, CCC-SLP & Diane Zajac, LMSW

Autism and Employment: Raising Your Child with Foundational Skills for the Future

All marketing and publishing rights guaranteed to and reserved by:

FUTURE HORIZONS INC.

721 W Abram St, Arlington, TX 76013

800-489-0727 (toll free)

817-277-0727 (local)

817-277-2270 (fax)

E-mail: *info@fhautism.com*

www.fhautism.com

ISBN: 9781941765814

CONTENTS

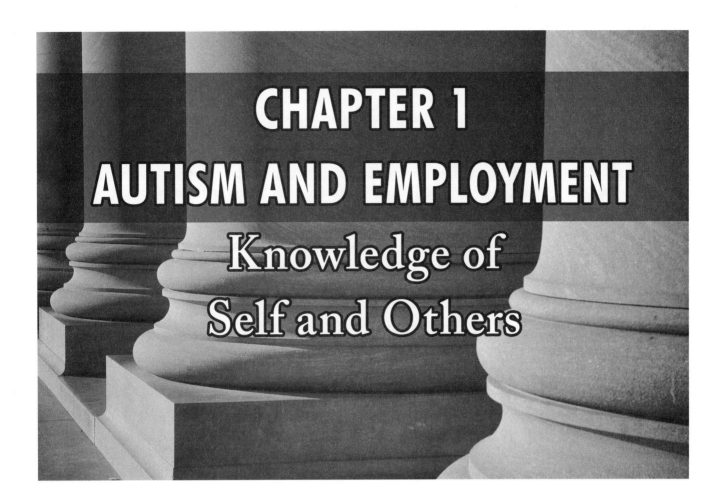

CHAPTER 1
AUTISM AND EMPLOYMENT
Knowledge of Self and Others

A s a parent, you want to ensure that your bright child with autism spectrum disorder will have a bright future! And you are not alone. According to an Easter Seals survey, parents of children who have ASD were most worried about their children having independence in adulthood. Quality of life, fitting into society, and employment were also top concerns. Your knowledge of your child, your devotion, and your many varied experiences with your child make you the ideal coach. This book was written to help you, the parent, to raise your child with the foundational skills he or she will need for the future.

Your child with ASD is a unique individual with many strengths. But we know that, by definition, children with ASD all have some degree of weakness in social-communication skills. Social-communication problems are a defining feature of ASD and include difficulties with social interaction (social reasoning, interacting with peers, resolving conflicts), social tasks (joining in with peers and cooperative play), social cognition (making inferences, regulating emotions, understanding social situations), and pragmatics (appropriate verbal expression, body language, eye contact). We can expect that all children with ASD will struggle in at least some of these areas. An individual with ASD may not make eye contact with those speaking to him, may not acknowledge others if they say hello, may say things that are not tactful, or may even inadvertently hurt the feelings of others. Your child with ASD may not understand jokes easily, he may misread body language as having an opposite meaning from the intended meaning, might say private things in a public group setting, or have a "meltdown" over a disagreement instead of negotiating a better outcome. Often, a child with ASD cannot accurately read the body language of others or projects body language that looks as if she is "uninterested" in others, impeding the development of friendships. When children with ASD interact with classmates, they may show less reciprocity, or "give and take," than their peers. For example, she might talk about her high-interest area rather than having a true social exchange with her classmate. Children with ASD may not fully appreciate or know how to respond to the feelings of others, particularly if the feelings are not the same as their own. Your child may not fully use gestures and may not engage in peer talk or use of slang. Your child with ASD may be very bright in most ways, but lack "common sense" in the social-communication realm.

Most concerning for you as a parent, social-communication skill deficits could impact your child's ability to become independent one day. Strong social-communication skills help individuals to interact productively and positively with others for any job. This is true even for high-tech jobs or jobs where the employee works from home. There must be phone calls, emails, meetings, group work on projects, marketing of products, interfacing with clients or buyers, problem solving for technical and other issues—all of which require communication with others. And as an independent adult, your child will also need to problem solve with others by using social communication beyond the workplace in order to obtain and maintain housing, manage finances, have relationships, drive, obtain benefits, and otherwise get his or her needs met.

The most important milestone for your child with ASD in terms of future independence will be to get and maintain employment! In 2014 it was estimated by the CDC that one in sixty-eight children had ASD, and Autism Speaks—an autism advocacy organization—estimated in June of 2012 that 500,000 teens and young adults with autism would be entering adulthood within the following ten years. These young adults with ASD will need paid employment to become independent. As a parent, you hope that your child can do paid work that is on a par with his or her cognitive and educational level and that is interesting and satisfying. The workplace is also where your child is likely to develop friendships and build self-esteem. It is vital to consider what it takes for your child with ASD to get and keep a job, and to make sure that she has those skills before she reaches adulthood and wants to enter the workforce.

There is a great deal of information available, on the internet and elsewhere, listing and describing the skills that employers want in their employees. Some of these skills, such as technical knowledge or critical thinking skills, are considered "hard skills," but in fact many or most of the desired employee attributes are social-communication, or "soft" skills.

Soft skills are those attributes of an individual that enhance their ability to interact positively and productively with others. For example, adaptability, dependability, communication, respect, responsibility, strong work ethic, confidence, and working well under pressure are all soft skills. For many soft skills, such as teamwork and collaboration, conflict resolution, and negotiation, social-communication skills are essential. There are some soft skills that are not clearly related to or supported by social-communication skills, such as dependability and strong work ethic, but for most of the crucial soft skills that promote positive employment outcomes in youth (discussed at length in the next chapter) an individual needs a strong foundation of social-communication skills.

Children with ASD often have many strengths that would be valued in the workplace. For example, your child may have good "hard skills," or technical expertise. He may have a special interest area that he is an expert in and go to college to specialize in a certain field of knowledge. However, the skills that employers identify as *most important or most lacking* in job applicants, generally, are the soft skills. Research indicates that soft skills, which include and are often supported by social-communication skills, are at least as important as technical skills as predictors for employment and earnings. Your child with ASD will be in competition with other young adults when he or she wants to enter the workforce. In competitive employment, where social-communication and soft skills are in demand, your child may struggle to win the job that he or she is otherwise qualified for.

One study looking at employment outcomes of young adults with ASD found that they worked fewer hours, were paid less, and had less varied occupations than individuals with other conditions. In fact, ASD youth were the least likely to have ever worked for pay. An Easter Seals survey in 2008 found that approximately six in ten individuals with ASD aged sixteen or older had not yet looked for work, while three-quarters of typically developing, same-age individuals were already working. Almost eight in ten young adults with autism were still living at home after high school, compared to slightly less than one-third of typically developing young adults.

Why have the employment outcomes for young adults with autism been so poor? If you consider the nature of ASD, which is largely defined by problems with social-communication skills, and the demands of employers for soft skills that are often very much dependent on social-communication skills, it becomes clear. How can you, as a parent, work toward a more positive outcome in adulthood for your child with ASD? How can you bring his or her social-communication and soft skills to the level required for success as an adult?

The first question you might ask is, "Can my child learn these skills at school?" Your child's public school is charged by the federal government with developing skills leading to successful employment and independence after high school through the IEP (individualized education program). This movement from high school to adult life is called "transition" in the IEP. The IEPs of all students aged sixteen and over are required to include "transition services," defined as "a coordinated set of activities for a child ... that focus on facilitating his/her movement from school to work and independent living." We can anticipate that, for children with ASD, one of the primary challenges in their transition after high school will be social communication. In addition to transition services through the IEP (for ages sixteen and above), your child may have social work and speech-language pathology services in school to address social-communication issues. However, given the broad needs that your child with ASD may have in this area, and with the background of academic and time pressure, school services may be unable to fully address all the non-academic needs your child has before he or she completes high school. Also, school is only one kind of environment. A child's life outside of school with parents, family, and friends has the greatest variety of contexts and situations and the best potential for the most effective practice of social-communication and soft skills.

At school, there is naturally an emphasis on academic learning and you may find that your child with ASD is a good student who excels in academic areas. He or she may be an expert in a certain subject area and you may well anticipate college for your child, or some other career-related training or education after high school. Will going to college or other post-secondary educational experience buy time for your child to develop the needed skills and set him up for success in employment? While more time for maturation may be helpful, it is unlikely to resolve the issue of developing soft skills to the degree necessary. If simple maturation and social experience could develop social-communication and soft skills to the level that is needed, your child would not have those deficit areas relative to peers now, nor indeed a diagnosis of ASD. We know from research that social-communication and soft skills are predictive of success in life and have a significant impact on employment outcomes. Even if your child with ASD is bright academically, and perhaps especially if he or she is, there needs to be a strong focus on developing those social-communication and soft skills to maximize his or her potential in adulthood.

The social-communication skills that are highlighted in this book are the foundational underpinnings of certain soft skills which have been shown to be the most crucial for positive employment outcomes in young people. We will discuss those skills and related issues in detail in the next chapter. The necessary social-communication skills are, for the most part, inherently difficult to master for many individuals with ASD and require specific practice at a foundational level over an extended period of time in a variety of contexts. You as the parent have the greatest knowledge of your child, the greatest investment in your child developing into a productive and happy adult, and the most influence on it. You have contact with your child continuously over many years in a variety of different situations; you have the best teachable moments! You can assist your child in gaining these skills, but you are likely to need guidance in deciding which skills to target and how to do it. This book is designed to help you take a systematic approach to your child's development in those areas that are likely to impact his or her future the most.

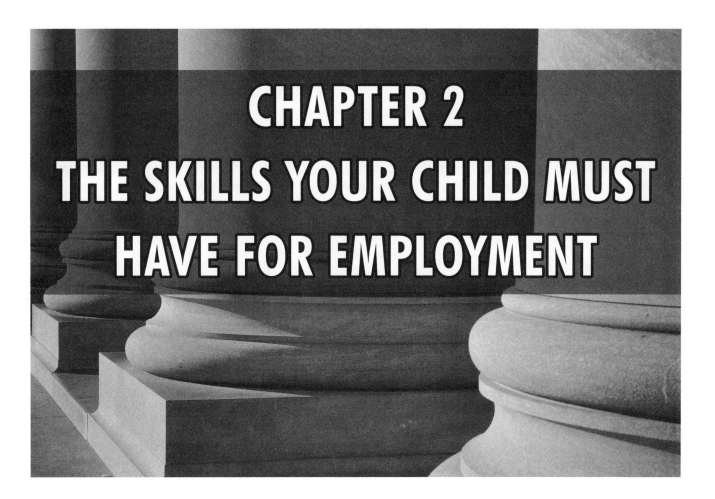

CHAPTER 2
THE SKILLS YOUR CHILD MUST HAVE FOR EMPLOYMENT

In Chapter One, we talked about the importance of soft skills for gaining employment, the relationship of social-communication skills to soft skills, the defining problems in these areas for individuals with ASD, and the statistics on employment for this group which are indicators of what needs to be done. In this chapter, we will outline the key soft skills that increase the chances for success in the workplace for young adults and identify specific foundational social-communication skills that support those soft skills. Chapters Three and Four will help you, the parent, in developing those social-communication skills to help your child to achieve employment and independence as a young adult. As noted earlier, the skills that allow a young person to attain employment, rather than just academic success, are the most crucial elements for future independence, as academic success does not necessarily predict employment success. Successful employment leads to independence! Since ASD is a condition that very particularly impacts social-communication skills, those skills will likely require explicit attention for a long time and across multiple contexts to make improvements substantial enough to develop the soft skills needed for employment. You, the parent, are in the best position to do this most effectively.

There is consensus among researchers that "soft skills" (which include social-communication skills) are at least as important as technical skills as predictors for employment and earnings. Employers are looking for soft skills even for highly technical jobs. But there are a wide variety of soft skills: good communication skills, positive attitude, teamwork, adaptability, dependability, responsibility, strong work ethic, confidence, working well under pressure, conflict resolution, writing skills, organizational skills, and so forth. Which soft skills are the ones most likely to increase the chances that a young adult will be successful in the workplace?

One group of researchers attempted to answer this question by conducting an extensive review of more than 380 resources from around the world looking at how soft skills impacted employment outcomes. They also looked at a broad spectrum of research on the topic and got input from other researchers, supervisors, employers, and young adults themselves. Their research yielded the following set of five key soft skills that appeared to increase the chances for success in the workplace for youth ages fifteen to nineteen:

1) Social skills
- Respecting others
- Using context-appropriate behavior
- Resolving conflict

2) Communication skills
- Oral
- Written
- Non-verbal
- Listening

3) Higher-order thinking
(includes the ability to identify an issue, and reach a conclusion after considering all the information and evaluating options)
- Problem solving
- Critical thinking
- Decision-making

4) Self-control

(leads to successful decision-making, resolution of conflict, and clear communication)

- Delay gratification
- Control impulses
- Direct and focus attention
- Manage emotions
- Regulate behaviors

5) A positive self-concept

- Self-confidence
- Self-efficacy
- Self-awareness and beliefs
- Self-esteem
- A sense of well-being and pride

As the parent of a child with ASD, you know that he may have difficulties with social skills, communication, higher-order thinking skills (including problem solving, critical thinking, and decision-making), self-control, and positive self-concept. Yet developing these soft skills is critical because they are the very ones that are most likely to help your child achieve and maintain employment, leading to independence. How can you teach these very broad skill sets? Let's start by examining the individual social-communication skills that make up and/or support these soft skills.

In considering the above categories and the soft skills listed, it is evident that the individual skills listed under each category could be broken down further, that is, they actually require the support of even more basic foundational skills. For example, "respecting others" would first require understanding that others may not feel the same way that the individual with ASD does, that all of us have our own feelings and beliefs, and that differences from one's own are acceptable. Understanding that others have their own feelings and beliefs is referred to as "theory of mind," an area of social cognition or emotional intelligence. Individuals with ASD may have difficulty with this concept, and they may struggle to comprehend the beliefs, attitudes, and emotions of other people. So, for children with ASD, we cannot just assume that they have the foundational social-communication skills that are needed to demonstrate "respecting others" in the workplace. To know that others have different beliefs and feelings than oneself and to be able to express acceptance of such differences requires first knowing *one's own* beliefs and feelings, i.e. one's own preferences and opinions, and we would expand this to include strengths and weaknesses. From this base, you can teach that others may differ in these areas and that this is quite normal and acceptable, and you can practice demonstrating or expressing acceptance of others. These are foundational social-communication skills that support conflict resolution, problem solving, and other soft skill areas in addition to "respecting others."

Although the soft skills "communication" and "social" are listed separately, functionally those and most of the other soft skills are supported by or stem from many of the same social-communication skills. The skills of impulse control, delaying gratification, and attention focus are possible exceptions to this, although the category "self-control" leads to successful decision-making, resolution of conflict, and clear communication. In other words, that category of "self-control" is partly a product of, or at least mediated by, social communication.

Let us consider other ways that social-communication skills support the five key soft skills. It is evident that how you comprehend and express body language impacts both whether you are able to perceive the needs of others by observing their body language (which supports, for example, resolving conflict and problem solving), and also whether you are able to accurately express your own feelings through your body language (which again supports resolving conflict, problem solving, and even self-confidence). How can a young adult with ASD know what the issues are that need to be solved if he can't read the body language of others, and how is her boss going to know that she is confident or respectful if she fails to express this non-verbally? In order to use context-appropriate behavior, an individual must be able to comprehend both the verbal and nonverbal features of the context; again, he or she must appreciate where other people are coming from, and also know how to blend in with others.

Clearly, the underpinnings and the functional expression in social contexts of the crucial soft skills listed above are "social communication" in nature. We know that these skills will be difficult for children with ASD to develop without targeted interventions. Each of these soft skills is largely the culmination of several foundational social-communication skills that we can identify, list, and target for improvement.

In Table One, you will see two sets of foundational skills divided into two categories: "knowledge of self and others" and "personal presentation skills." They were selected because they are all basic social-communication skills (except for grooming/hygiene/dress, which will be discussed later) that youth with ASD may struggle with, and they are necessary supports for the larger soft skills identified by research as being most crucial to positive employment outcomes (as shown in Table Two).

You will note in Table Two that for each of the soft skills listed, supporting foundational social-communication skills are also listed—often several of them. For example, there are seventeen foundational skills that support respect. For brevity and clarity of presentation, some skills are listed in combined fashion, e.g., "accurately expresses a variety of feeling words, both positive and negative, for his own feelings and those of others" combines skills that are closely related. Also "expressing," or showing knowledge of a skill, is grouped with "demonstrating" for the purposes of this table ("*expresses and demonstrates* appropriate perspective on a variety of problems"), although in fact they are not quite the same thing. Your child may be able to verbally express what "perspective" means because she understands the concept, but she may not in fact demonstrate it at the required moment. Generally, it is easier and quicker to learn to express a concept verbally than it is to demonstrate a skill. Verbal expression is a way to gauge understanding; it is how you will know that your child understands the skill concept, so it is very important. Understanding and expressing that understanding verbally is the first step, and sets the stage for development of the use or demonstration of the skill in real life situations.

CHAPTER 2 The Skills Your Child Must Have

Table One

FOUNDATIONAL SOCIAL-COMMUNICATION SKILLS
Knowledge of Self and Others (KSO) Skills

1. Positively expresses personal preferences and opinions
2. Positively expresses strengths and weaknesses
3. Accurately expresses a variety of feeling words, both positive and negative, for own feelings and those of others
4. Accurately describes and positively frames ASD
5. Expresses and demonstrates self-acceptance
6. Expresses and demonstrates accepting others
7. Expresses and demonstrates appropriate perspective on a variety of problems

Personal Presentation (PP) Skills

1. Stays within personal space appropriately
2. Shows appropriate body language while listening
3. Reads the body language of others
4. Expresses positive body language when communicating
5. Acknowledges and responds to others
6. Attempts to blend in with others
7. Independent with appropriate and positive personal presentation: grooming, hygiene, dress
8. Uses positive word choices (kind talk, positive self-talk, polite talk, encouragement, compliments, tact, appropriate talk for time/place/person)
9. Demonstrates flexibility when unexpected things happen
10. Communicates positively to problem-solve with others

Table Two

THE FIVE KEY SOFT SKILLS (Lipman, Ryberg, Carney, Moore, 2015)
With supporting foundational social-communication skills from Table One

1. SOCIAL SKILLS

RESPECTING OTHERS

Positively expresses personal preferences and opinions

Positively expresses strengths and weaknesses

Accurately describes and positively frames ASD

Accurately expresses a variety of feeling words, both positive and negative, for own feelings and those of others

Expresses and demonstrates self-acceptance

Expresses and demonstrates accepting others

Expresses and demonstrates appropriate perspective on a variety of problems

Attempts to blend in with others

Shows appropriate body language while listening

Stays within personal space appropriately

Expresses positive body language when communicating

Reads the body language of others

Acknowledges and responds to others

Uses positive word choices (kind talk, positive self-talk, polite talk, encouragement, compliments, tact, appropriate talk for time/place/person)

Independent with appropriate and positive personal presentation: grooming, hygiene, dress

Demonstrates flexibility when unexpected things happen

Communicates positively to problem-solve with others

THE FIVE KEY SOFT SKILLS (continued)

USING CONTEXT-APPROPRIATE BEHAVIOR

Positively expresses personal preferences, opinions

Positively expresses strengths and weaknesses

Accurately describes and positively frames ASD

Accurately expresses a variety of feeling words, both positive and negative, for own feelings and those of others

Expresses and demonstrates self-acceptance

Expresses and demonstrates accepting others

Expresses and demonstrates appropriate perspective on a variety of problems

Attempts to blend in with others

Shows appropriate body language while listening

Stays within personal space appropriately

Expresses positive body language when communicating

Reads the body language of others

Acknowledges and responds to others

Uses positive word choices (kind talk, positive self-talk, polite talk, encouragement, compliments, tact, appropriate talk for time/place/person)

Demonstrates flexibility when unexpected things happen

Communicates positively to problem-solve with others

RESOLVING CONFLICT

Positively expresses personal preferences, opinions

Positively expresses strengths and weaknesses

Accurately describes and positively frames ASD

Accurately expresses a variety of feeling words, both positive and negative, for own feelings and those of others

Expresses and demonstrates self-acceptance

THE FIVE KEY SOFT SKILLS (continued)

Expresses and demonstrates accepting others

Expresses and demonstrates appropriate perspective on a variety of problems

Attempts to blend in with others

Shows appropriate body language while listening

Stays within personal space appropriately

Expresses positive body language when communicating

Reads the body language of others

Acknowledges and responds to others

Uses positive word choices (kind talk, positive self-talk, polite talk, encouragement, compliments, tact, appropriate talk for time/place/person)

Demonstrates flexibility when unexpected things happen

Communicates positively to problem-solve with others

2. COMMUNICATION SKILLS

ORAL AND WRITTEN (COMBINED)

Positively expresses personal preferences, opinions

Positively expresses strengths and weaknesses

Accurately describes and positively frames ASD

Expresses a variety of feeling words, both positive and negative, for own feelings and those of others

Expresses and demonstrates self-acceptance

Expresses and demonstrates accepting others

Expresses and demonstrates appropriate perspective on a variety of problems

Attempts to blend in with others

Acknowledges and responds to others

Uses positive word choices (kind talk, positive self-talk, polite talk, encouragement, compliments, tact, appropriate talk for time/place/person)

THE FIVE KEY SOFT SKILLS (continued)

Demonstrates flexibility when unexpected things happen

Communicates positively to problem-solve with others

NON-VERBAL

Expresses and demonstrates self-acceptance

Expresses and demonstrates accepting others

Expresses and demonstrates appropriate perspective on a variety of problems

Attempts to blend in with others

Shows appropriate body language while listening

Stays within personal space appropriately

Expresses positive body language when communicating

Reads the body language of others (including facial expression)

Acknowledges and responds to others

Independent with appropriate and positive personal presentation: grooming, hygiene, dress

Demonstrates flexibility when unexpected things happen

LISTENING

Attempts to blend in with others

Shows appropriate body language while listening

Stays within personal space appropriately

Expresses positive body language (including facial expression) when communicating

Reads the body language of others (including facial expression)

Acknowledges and responds to others

THE FIVE KEY SOFT SKILLS (continued)

3. HIGHER ORDER THINKING

(includes the ability to identify an issue and reach a conclusion after considering all the information and evaluating options)

PROBLEM SOLVING

Positively expresses personal preference, opinions

Positively expresses strengths and weaknesses

Accurately describes and positively frames ASD

Accurately expresses a variety of feeling words, both positive and negative, for own feelings and those of others

Expresses and demonstrates self-acceptance

Expresses and demonstrates accepting others

Expresses and demonstrates appropriate perspective on a variety of problems

Attempts to blend in with others

Shows appropriate body language while listening

Stays within personal space appropriately

Expresses positive body language when communicating

Reads the body language of others

Acknowledges and responds to others

Uses positive word choices (kind talk, positive self-talk, polite talk, encouragement, compliments, tact, appropriate talk for time/place/person)

Demonstrates flexibility when unexpected things happen

Communicates positively to problem-solve with others

CRITICAL THINKING

Positively expresses personal preference, opinions

Positively expresses strengths and weaknesses

THE FIVE KEY SOFT SKILLS (continued)

Accurately describes and positively frames ASD

Accurately expresses a variety of feeling words, both positive and negative, for own feelings and those of others

Expresses and demonstrates self-acceptance

Expresses and demonstrates accepting others

Expresses and demonstrates appropriate perspective on a variety of problems

Attempts to blend in with others

Reads the body language of others (including facial expression)

Communicates positively to problem-solve with others

DECISION-MAKING

Positively expresses personal preference, opinions

Positively expresses strengths and weaknesses

Accurately describes and positively frames ASD

Accurately expresses a variety of feeling words, both positive and negative, for own feelings and those of others

Expresses and demonstrates self-acceptance

Expresses and demonstrates accepting others

Expresses and demonstrates appropriate perspective on a variety of problems

Attempts to blend in with others

Shows appropriate body language while listening

Stays within personal space appropriately

Expresses positive body language when communicating

Reads the body language of others

Acknowledges and responds to others

Uses positive word choices (kind talk, positive self-talk, polite talk, encouragement, compliments, tact, appropriate talk for time/place/person)

Independent with appropriate and positive personal presentation: grooming, hygiene, dress

Demonstrates flexibility when unexpected things happen

Communicates positively to problem-solve with others

4. SELF-CONTROL

(leads to successful decision-making, resolution of conflict, and clear communication)

- Delay gratification

- Control impulses

- Direct and focus attention

- Manage emotions

- Regulate behaviors

For all of the above:

Positively expresses personal preference, opinions

Positively expresses strengths and weaknesses

Accurately describes and positively frames ASD

Accurately expresses a variety of feeling words, both positive and negative, for own feelings and those of others

Expresses and demonstrates self-acceptance

Expresses and demonstrates accepting others

Expresses and demonstrates appropriate perspective on a variety of problems

Attempts to blend in with others

Shows appropriate body language while listening

Stays within personal space appropriately

Expresses positive body language when communicating

Acknowledges and responds to others

Uses positive word choices (kind talk, positive self-talk, polite talk, encouragement, compliments, tact, appropriate talk for time/place/person)

Demonstrates flexibility when unexpected things happen

Communicates positively to problem-solve with others

5. A POSITIVE SELF-CONCEPT

- Self-confidence

- Self-efficacy

- Self-awareness and beliefs

- Self-esteem

- A sense of well-being and pride

For all of the above:

Positively expresses personal preference, opinions

Positively expresses strengths and weaknesses

Accurately describes and positively frames ASD

Accurately expresses a variety of feeling words, both positive and negative, for own feelings and those of others

Expresses and demonstrates self-acceptance

Expresses and demonstrates accepting others

Expresses and demonstrates appropriate perspective on a variety of problems

Attempts to blend in with others

Stays within personal space appropriately

Expresses positive body language (including facial expression) when communicating

Acknowledges and responds to others

Uses positive word choices (kind talk, positive self-talk, polite talk, encouragement, compliments, tact, appropriate talk for time/place/person)

Independent with appropriate and positive personal presentation: grooming, hygiene, dress

Demonstrates flexibility when unexpected things happen

Communicates positively to problem-solve with others

The foundational skills were selected because they are both 1) social-communication skills that support each of the desired soft skills and 2) skills that are expected to be weak in individuals with ASD. It is worth noting that even for individuals without ASD, the extent to which one develops full competency in these skills will depend upon many factors, including personality, environment, exposure, and of course, age. However, for your child who has ASD, the foundational skills may not develop fully because ASD is largely an impairment of social-communication skills. For your child, these skills should be addressed systematically and long-term, with a view toward incorporating the understanding and use of them into the fabric of your child's daily life; this is the focus of Chapters Three and Four. The ultimate goal is for your child to develop the soft skills that are needed for employment, independence, and relationships in adulthood.

You will note that the foundational skills are divided into "knowledge of self and others" and "personal presentation." These were natural groupings based on the nature of the foundational skill content. In our experience, "knowledge of self and others" along with "theory of mind" issues in autism provides necessary support for "personal presentation skills." If you do not have awareness and acceptance of the differences between yourself and others in feelings, opinions, and so forth, then you will not be able to effectively blend (project the appropriate body language and be able to read theirs, choose the appropriate words to say, and problem solve with them). Knowledge and acceptance of themselves and others will help individuals with ASD to be flexible when unexpected things happen, to problem solve, care for themselves, desire to present themselves positively, and to acknowledge others rather than retreating or feeling uncomfortable. The opposite is also true, that personal presentation skills reinforce positivity and deepen knowledge of self and others; however, everything begins with positive knowledge and acceptance of yourself and others. Knowledge of self and others are crucial skills that often do not come easily for children with ASD due to theory of mind issues and anxiety, and in our opinion need the most primary and ongoing attention of the two sets of foundational skills.

Positivity is a common theme all through the foundational skills and merits some discussion. It is clear when you look at the soft skills, and it is common sense, that employers (and friends!) are looking for people who are positive. It happens sometimes that children with ASD respond to their anxiety and difficulties in social situations with negativity. In general, it is our experience that negativity magnifies the social issues that a child with ASD struggles with, and that conflicts and difficulties are reduced or even eliminated by positivity. We would urge you, as a general rule and habit, to frame others, interactions with others (and potentially misinterpreted interactions with others), "triggers" for behaviors, life's mishaps, setbacks, unexpected events, and social situations in general positively. It may be an uphill fight against the anxiety, but it will pay off. Your child is most likely to be successful in learning and applying the foundational social-communication skills if he or she operates from a base of positivity. You will see tools, activities, and verbiage specifically addressing positivity in Chapter Three.

Positivity also means sharing and positively framing information related to his medical diagnosis or school eligibility of autism spectrum disorder with your child. Your child's understanding of and ability to express issues related to his ASD is a foundational skill that supports the soft skills. Your child knows that she struggles and is liable to feel anxious about her differences from others. Before she begins to doubt, criticize, or blame herself or others in an effort to cope, give her the understanding. Let her feel frustrated with the ASD, but love and accept herself and her unique qualities! It is essential for many of the foundational skills for her to have this positive understanding of herself; in order to accept others and come to understand them, she must first accept and understand

herself. We believe that knowledge of ASD and a positive, adaptive response to it will lead to success with the soft skills of respect, problem-solving, using context-appropriate behaviors, resolving conflict, and many more. Also, as an adult in a work environment, she may need to request accommodations such as breaks or get help in dealing with others when there are conflicts. Being able to positively articulate her unique issues and needs as an individual with ASD allows her to self-advocate and to obtain help from others as needed.

You may note that one of the foundational skills under "personal presentation" is not technically a social-communication skill. "Independent with appropriate and positive personal presentation: grooming, hygiene, dress" was included because it is so integral to body language and to success in employment. "Showing appropriate body language" is very much supported by appropriate grooming, hygiene, and dress. Independence in this is a skill that supports positive body language, success in employment, and is basic to the category concept of personal presentation.

At this point you may be asking yourself, "Where does my child stand with respect to those foundational skills?" There are multiple points to consider! As noted previously, these are all skills that individuals with ASD will likely struggle with; however, some children with ASD have milder social-communication issues than others, and there are factors of personality, environment, cognition, experience, and age that influence how difficult it may be to acquire the skills. Regarding the skills themselves, there are multiple elements involved in fully achieving them. For example, there is a difference between expressing (or showing) knowledge of a skill and demonstrating it. Your child may be able to express what tact is because she understands the concept, but she may not use tact when speaking with others. Your child must ultimately be able to demonstrate the social-communication skills as well as verbally express what they are. Skills must also occur with the appropriate frequency; it is not enough, for example, for a young adult to "acknowledge and respond to others" only on rare occasion. The skills must also occur at the appropriate time and place, and with the right people. Your child must understand why a skill is important in order for him or her to choose it and use it at the right time with the right people. The skills must occur across contexts—he should not only display the skill appropriately in one kind of situation, but wherever it is called for. Moreover, the skills must often occur with each other, i.e., positive word choices need to be expressed with matching positive body language. These many facets of skill development will be referred to in the following chapters as "elements" of the skills. Finally, there is the issue of whether your child is doing the skill with help (prompting, reminding, cueing, modeling) or without help (independently, without cues). For example, perhaps your child stays within her own personal space with others when you prompt her to, but does not do so consistently without reminders. To be functional in an employment setting, your child must ultimately do the skills independently.

Before introducing these skills to your child (Chapter Three), it may be helpful to you to understand what the "end product" is, what each skill should look like when the above elements of appropriate frequency, independence, skill coordination, etc. are included. Table Three attempts to describe the foundational skills at this end level, with consideration for the elements needed for full and complete skill development. Please don't feel discouraged as you look at the end-level skill development. Remember that your child with ASD starts with issues in social-communication skills, and progress may be slow and uneven, but he or she can and will continue to improve and grow in these skills with your support.

Table Three

DESCRIPTION OF END-LEVEL FOUNDATIONAL SOCIAL-COMMUNICATION SKILLS

A. KNOWLEDGE OF SELF AND OTHERS

1. **My child positively expresses personal preferences/opinions.**

   Does he enjoy sports or prefer to watch TV? Does he like to go camping with the family, or does he prefer to stay indoors? Would he rather be with a group of people or alone? Does he want to live in the city or in the country? Does he think that cats are smarter than dogs? Does he think math is easier than reading a book?

   Your child knows his own preferences and opinions and is able to describe and share them with a positive or neutral voice tone, at the right time and place, and with the right person/people at an appropriate frequency. He understands that what he likes is unique to him, that everyone has preferences and opinions, that those are likely different than his, that they are not good or bad, and that knowledge of his own preferences makes him able to make positive choices that are right for him.

2. **My child positively expresses strengths and weaknesses.**

   Is she good in math but weaker in reading comprehension? Does she get uncomfortable in crowds

DESCRIPTION OF ... SOCIAL-COMMUNICATION SKILLS (continued)

but feels confident when with family? Does she struggle to know what to say to peers but is a kind and loyal friend? Does she get upset easily but always says she is sorry?

Your child can easily and comfortably express her strengths and weaknesses without being upset or defensive and with a neutral voice tone and appropriate body language. She does so at the right time and place, and with the right person/people. She knows that she sometimes needs help for weaknesses and is comfortable asking for help and explaining why she needs it. She might volunteer to help others in a strength area for her. She knows that her strengths and weaknesses are unique to her, that everyone has them and those of other people are different than her own, and that they are not good or bad. She understands that she will improve in areas of weakness and that others can help her. She can express why knowing about her strengths and weaknesses is important.

3. **My child accurately expresses a variety of "feeling" words, both positive and negative, in a variety of situations, for his or her own feelings and those of others.**

His vocabulary of negative and positive feeling words is large and diverse. He and other people don't feel just "bad," "mad," "fine," or "good"; rather they are "frustrated," "anxious," "excited," "embarrassed," "exhausted," "worried," "proud," etc. He expresses feelings at the right time and place, with the right person/people, and with appropriate body language and intensity. He can accurately and positively describe his feelings verbally as well as the behaviors that may be associated with them. He can share feelings so others can help him with them. He knows that how other people feel about things is unique to them, is likely to be different than how he feels, and that it is not good or bad. He can accurately and positively describe the feelings of others verbally and is aware of the behaviors that may be associated with them. He will listen to others expressing their feelings and is supportive and understanding of them. He can express why this is important.

4. **My child accurately describes and positively frames ASD.**

She understands that she has a diagnosis, or school eligibility for special education, of ASD. She thinks of it in terms of strengths and weaknesses, and knows which areas are difficult for her and which things about her own version of ASD make her unique and special. She expresses this at the right time and place, and with the right person/people. When she is upset or embarrassed about her behavior, or frustrated with some aspect of ASD that she is dealing with, she thinks of it as a weaker area that can and will improve. She understands that others can help her and seeks and accepts their help. She understands that others love and care about her just the way she is and support her. She can express why knowing about her ASD is important.

5. **My child expresses and demonstrates self-acceptance.**

He knows and expresses that he is unique, and that it is okay because everyone is different. He expresses this at the right time and place, with the right person/people, and with appropriate body language and voice tone. He knows that he has ASD, like so many other children and adults, and that

DESCRIPTION OF ... SOCIAL-COMMUNICATION SKILLS (continued)

he has weaknesses like everyone else. He does not judge these negatively but accepts them for what they are, and knows he can and will improve in areas that he would like to make positive changes in. He demonstrates respect for himself in the things he does. He can express why this is important.

6. **My child expresses and demonstrates accepting others.**

She knows that everyone has their own opinions, preferences, strengths, and weaknesses, and she expresses this positively. She expresses that these are not good or bad, just different. She expresses this at the right time and place, with the right person/people, and appropriate body language. She can talk about differences with others non-judgmentally and respectfully, with a positive or neutral voice tone and tact. She responds appropriately and respectfully to others, even if she does not agree with them, and can express why this is important.

7. **My child expresses and demonstrates appropriate perspective on a variety of problems.**

He has a variety of ways that he thinks about problems. He knows that "sometimes these things just happen," sometimes "things are just an accident or a mistake," and can forgive himself and others. He recognizes and is sensitive to the feelings that someone might have in a variety of situations, such as their possible embarrassment. He expresses his own feelings appropriately, at the right time and place, with the right person/people, and with appropriate body language. He uses tools if he needs them to help him to get and maintain perspective. Blame is appropriately placed, if at all. He recognizes how his behavior, misreading the situation, etc. might have contributed to the problem, as appropriate. He shows anger only when something is intentionally done to hurt or bother him and deals with it appropriately (requests for the person to stop the behavior, asks another person for assistance, etc.). He is able to rank the intensity of his feelings on a scale (zero to four) about the problem, in an appropriate range. He knows why it is important to have perspective on problems.

B. PERSONAL PRESENTATION SKILLS

1. **My child stays within his own personal space appropriately.**

My child respects personal boundaries around others. He understands that everyone has an invisible "bubble" around them that is their own space, and that they usually don't like it if someone is inside that space with them (with the exception to this is family members and very close friends). He knows that this helps others to feel comfortable so they can focus on what they are saying and doing, and that it also makes others want to be around him.

2. **My child shows appropriate body language while listening.**

My child has the following behavior while listening: sits upright, shoulders are turned to face the speaker with her body, makes eye contact, and has a friendly and interested expression on her face.

DESCRIPTION OF ... SOCIAL-COMMUNICATION SKILLS (continued)

Hands, legs, and body are still. She understands that good listening body language shows respect and interest in others.

3. **My child reads the body language of others.**

   She understands that the words a person says do not carry all the meaning. She looks carefully at the bodies and faces of people to help her know what they mean when they are talking. If she is not sure of the meaning, she asks someone she can trust. She can tell why this is important.

4. **My child expresses positive body language when communicating.**

   When talking to others, he makes eye contact and stands or sits upright with his body facing them to show interest and respect. His facial expression is pleasant and friendly while speaking. His voice tone is appropriate. He can verbalize the importance of positive body language when he is communicating with others.

5. **My child acknowledges and responds to others.**

   If someone looks at him and smiles, he smiles back and/or replies verbally. If they wave or nod, he waves or nods back or replies verbally. If he is spoken to, he says something back. If he is asked a question he answers it if he can, otherwise he says that he doesn't know the answer (instead of saying nothing). He knows that acknowledging others is polite and shows respect and interest.

6. **My child tries to blend in with others.**

   In group settings, he looks to see how other people are speaking and acting and he tries to match their behaviors. He recognizes that other people notice how he talks and acts, and that they may judge him by his behavior. He recognizes that if he is doing or saying what others are not, this could be inappropriate. He knows it is important for others to make positive judgments about him and tries to blend in with them.

7. **My child is independent with appropriate and positive personal presentation: grooming, hygiene, dress.**

   Your child grooms herself carefully and appropriately. She makes sure she is clean at the appropriate time and frequency. She dresses herself appropriately for the setting and activity.

8. **My child uses positive word choices:**

   KIND TALK

   Your child says kind things to other people if they are having a hard time or just to be friendly. For example, "I'm sorry that happened," "I hope you have fun this weekend," or "Do you want to share some of my lunch?" He understands that this helps him to make friends and to have a good reputation with others.

POSITIVE SELF-TALK

When she is worried, nervous, or scared, she says encouraging things to herself. For example, "Just a little more and I will be done," "Good job," or "I can do it." She knows this can help her cope with anxiety and persist despite problems.

POLITE TALK

Your child says "please," "thank you," and "excuse me" at the appropriate times. He uses appropriate body language and voice tone when saying these things. He knows this is respectful and friendly.

ENCOURAGEMENT

When someone she knows is worried, nervous, or scared, she says encouraging things to them. For example, "Keep trying," "Good job," or "You can do it!" She uses appropriate body language and voice tone when saying these things. She knows this can help her build friendships and be a good team player.

COMPLIMENTS

Your child compliments someone when they do something well, look nice, or do something kind, with appropriate voice tone and body language. He can say why this is important.

TACT

Your child chooses words carefully so as to not hurt anyone's feelings or sound rude or bossy. She understands that she doesn't always need to say the exact truth, some things do not need to be said at all, and above all she must consider people's feelings before she speaks. She considers the Commenting Rule (described later in the text) to help her know what to say. She understands why it is important.

APPROPRIATE TALK—TIME/PLACE/PERSON

Your child understands that she addresses strangers differently than people she knows, and friends differently from authority figures. She may use different words and a different tone of voice with each group. She picks the right time and place to talk, that is, she does not interrupt and makes sure that private things are said in a private place. She speaks to the right person about the right matters and she speaks about private things only with known and trusted people. She can tell why it is important.

9. **My child demonstrates flexibility when unexpected things happen.**

   When unexpected things happen, your child can cope and change with the situation. She may have special ways or tools to relax and feel less frustrated or anxious, and uses them in an unobtrusive way. She can use tools to help her maintain perspective. She maintains a calm voice and seeks help if needed. She does not blame others.

10. **My child communicates positively to problem-solve with others.**

    He accepts responsibility to solve problems on his own or for helping others to solve problems. He communicates with others when he encounters a problem. He communicates with the right person/people at the right time and place about a problem, with appropriate body language and voice tone. He does not blame others but looks for help if he needs it, and cooperates with others in finding a solution to the problem. He stays patient and calm and uses positive words to describe what he is thinking and feeling. He considers what kind of problem it is, and uses tools as needed to help him maintain perspective. He understands that others depend on him to work to solve problems.

CHAPTER 3
INTRODUCING THE FOUNDATIONAL SOCIAL-COMMUNICATION SKILLS

In Chapter Two, you learned about a set of five key soft skills that have been shown to enhance employment outcomes for youth; the social-communication skills that support development of those soft skills are the subject of this book. Those social-communication skills were described as foundational and were divided into two groups: knowledge of self and others, and personal presentation. Skills under "knowledge of self and others" address theory of mind issues (described earlier) head on, and are foundational to almost all the soft skills and many of the social-communication skills in the "personal presentation" skill set as well. As described previously, all the social-communication skills that are needed for the critical soft skills are expected to be difficult for children with ASD, although there are factors that might make them more or less so, such as the degree of impact of the autism, age, experience, personality, and so forth. In this chapter you will be given concepts for each of the skills to share with your child with verbiage to help define them, tools, talking points, and some activities. This will help your child to develop specifically the elements of verbally expressing the skills, telling why they are important, and demonstrating the skills with support. The other elements of the foundational skills, along with working toward independence and carryover generally, will be addressed in Chapter Four.

In introducing the foundational social-communication skills to your child, you will use a set of tools uniquely adapted for each of the skills.

These tools include:
- Continuum of preferences and opinions
- Continuum of strengths and weaknesses

- Strengths chart
- Intensity level for feelings
- Feelings chart
- Problem perspective
- Positivity

These tools in a "basic" version, i.e. without reference to a particular skill, can be found at the end of this chapter.

It is recommended that you work through each of the skills presented in this chapter in the order presented, since the concepts in prior skills will help to develop the concepts in subsequent skills—particularly in the "knowledge of self and others" area. A unit has been built around each skill that includes the tools for that skill, the suggested verbiage for defining and discussing the skills and for using the tools, some activities, and a "check out" to make sure that you and your child have covered the bases.

Ideally, after completing all the skills, you will be revisiting the concepts and using the tools throughout your lives together, developing more elements of each skill over time (see Chapter Four). The ideas offered in this chapter will be made more powerful by your knowledge of your child and the richness of experience that you as a parent are uniquely suited to provide.

In introducing the concepts and going through the skills, we are not going to be concerned with your child's beginning level, or indeed whether he or she has any concepts about the skill at all. We are going to assume that your child with ASD has delays or differences in his or her development of all these skills and that at least some of the elements for fully functional, independent use of these skills will be missing because of the nature of ASD. For your child, all of these foundational skills are highly likely to need to be better integrated with each other, to occur more often at the right time and place, to be used more independently, and so forth. The explicit introduction and the shared reference points and tools that you will be using in each of the units will be useful, regardless of your starting point as far as skill development. Also, one of the main points of working through each of these skills is developing shared reference points and tools that you can incorporate into your lives for the future. The shared concepts and tools can be used in new situations and to tackle new challenges. After working through each of the units, you should be able to take advantage of suggestions in Chapter Four to increase the number of skill elements and create carryover.

The activities, suggested verbiage and definitions, tools, and so forth of each unit in this chapter were designed to be universal and applicable regardless of age and whether or not he or she may already have some positive development in these social-communication skills. However, for younger or less mature children, those who also have very significant attention problems, behavior and/or emotional issues, or highly focused interests, you may need to modify the verbiage or selectively use the unit information and tools. You need to be flexible with how structured you are and how much time you are spending at once on them. While fifteen to twenty minutes of dedicated time for skill concepts might be optimal for an older or more focused child, this might not work for every child. How you introduce the skills and use the tools should reflect what you know about your child and the teachable moments that are unique to his or her life.

CHAPTER 3 Introducing the Foundational Skills

For example, if your child is younger or does better with just a little bit of information at a time and then needs time to process it, go with that. If your child gets anxious or oppositional, drop it and come back to it later or get around to it with teachable moments using the tools. For example, "Your little sister is so upset, which number on this scale do you think she is at (showing the intensity scale)? Let's see if we can help her get down to a one." "Wow, you are way at the other end of the continuum line compared to me, you really like videos, but you know I really like books better! I hope I get a book for Mother's Day!" If you slip the concepts and tools in as teachable moments now, you may be able to work through them in a more structured fashion when your child is older and more mature or more able to focus.

We would suggest that your child be at least seven years old for you to begin working with him or her with these skills; however, you may be able to start younger or you may even need to postpone working on the skills until your child has more maturity or better self-regulation. Ideally, you should be working on these skills by at least middle school, since the goal is for all of these skills to be as well-developed as possible by the time he or she is ready for employment. The years go by fast!

Please consider that your child with ASD may struggle to understand the big picture and to relate these concepts to what he wants now and in future. We suggest that you prioritize his learning these skills and work through them at minimum in a modified way, striving to reach a point where he can express understanding of them, tell why they are important, and show them with your guidance. Those are the goals of each of the skill units in this chapter. What do you do if, despite your best efforts, he habitually approaches learning these skills with negativity? Ultimately, once you get through all the skill units in some fashion, you will have reference points and tools to tackle negativity issues. If you need to do so, you could focus on positivity by itself using the strengths chart and referring to the strengths/weaknesses continuum line to talk about moving in the right direction. In addition to praise, you may want to offer tangible rewards for improved positivity. If negativity is a major problem with his ASD, maybe the whole family can participate and find themselves on the strengths continuum line for positivity, earning points for moving in the right direction and making improvements. Then, when the whole family improves their positivity enough, you can all go out and do a fun activity that your child with ASD has chosen.

Frequently, a child with a great deal of negative response to his challenges states that he feels angry when in fact it is frustration, anxiety, embarrassment, or some other uncomfortable feeling he is experiencing. The feelings vocabulary tool and Unit Three should help with that. Also, there is sometimes a desire by the child to blame others when he is experiencing an uncomfortable feeling; the problem perspective tool and Unit Seven may be helpful for this. During discussion about ASD, tactfully noting that he or she might be prone to misreading or misunderstanding others or social situations, and offering support for this, could be a useful insight to share in certain situations—especially for older children. Expressing and demonstrating acceptance of himself and others is a skill that you will be covering and persistently modeling this may be helpful. As noted earlier, once you get through all of the "knowledge of self and others" section you will have a great deal more tools and shared concepts to work with. We encourage you to persevere until you get through all the skill units, modified if you need to, and hopefully his or her insights will be developed through the course of it. You will have shared concepts and tools as touchstones, and you may turn the corner with positivity!

We recommend that you make these units a shared project of self-discovery and follow them up with fun activities. Going through the units could even be a shared project with siblings or other family members. Refer back to the skill concepts whenever the time is right, and incorporate the use of the tools into your everyday lives. Look for teachable moments! After you learn the concepts and the use of the tools you might say:

- "I am frustrated at about a number three right now and it's uncomfortable, I'm going to go be by myself for a while until I am feeling more like a one."
- "Cooking is just not something I like to do very much—I'm way down at this end of the continuum (point to place on the line). But I have to do it sometimes. Do you want to do it with me today to help make it more fun for me?"
- "Puzzles are a real strength for you! They are a weakness for me, maybe if you help me find pieces I will get better at it."
- "Do you need help? That might be a weaker area for you. It's pretty much a strength for me—let me see if I can help you out."
- "You really seem upset. Let's look at the feelings vocabulary to see if we can find just the right word that describes how you are feeling, and let's look at the feelings intensity scale so you can tell me what number you are on that, okay?"
- "Yeah, that's one of those ASD things that might trip you up, so we will be on the lookout for it next time, and I will help you get through it."
- "I know that feels a four to you, but your brother and I are feeling that only at a one, and here's why..."
- "Let's write the problem down and see where it goes on the problems perspective tool—was it really 'on purpose to hurt or bother you?'"

As a general rule for the purpose of this chapter and introducing all the skills, you will move on from one skill unit to the next when your child can define the skill concept of that unit, tell why it is important, and demonstrate it with some guidance from you. Each unit ends with a "check out" page for you to make sure you are ready to move on to the next unit. The definition of the skills includes at least one statement about why that skill is important, and you can modify or add more to better reflect your beliefs and lifestyle. Very often "respect" and "reputation" are included in talking about why the skills are important, and you can't over-emphasize these points! We sometimes call respect and reputation "the two R's."

Respect means thinking about and treating others in a thoughtful and positive manner. Our reputation is what people think and say about us by noticing what we do and say. It is important for your child

CHAPTER 3 Introducing the Foundational Skills

to understand, because he or she may not do so intuitively, that others are always noticing him and what kind of person he is: kind, bossy, mean, helpful, positive, negative, etc. It is our experience that children, including children with ASD, do really start to care about their reputation in middle school; by then, all children have had the experience of having to work in groups with other children that they didn't care for, and they don't want to be the person that no one wants to be in a group with! If you talk about why we care throughout these programs of "knowledge of self and others" and "personal presentation," referencing respect and reputation over and over again, your child may begin to internalize it.

Another concept occasionally referred to in the skill units is what we are calling "the commenting rule." This rule says that before you say something about someone else, you should consider whether it is nice and whether it is necessary to say. What your child says about others should typically be both nice and necessary. I encourage you to repeat the commenting rule in appropriate contexts in your life with your ASD child, perhaps connecting it with positivity, in hopes that he or she may internalize it and reflect on it independently before speaking.

Due to the fundamental nature of the concepts in knowledge of self and others, you should do your best to do all of the units in this area (even if you are unable to do anything else in this book)! Remember that for both areas, the point is for you to establish shared reference points, concepts, and tools that you can refer to often in multiple contexts over time. The skills and units are as follows:

Knowledge of Self and Others (KSO) Skills

1. Positively expresses personal preferences and opinions

2. Positively expresses strengths and weaknesses

3. Accurately expresses a variety of feeling words, both positive and negative, for own feelings and those of others

4. Accurately describes and positively frames ASD

5. Expresses and demonstrates self-acceptance

6. Expresses and demonstrates accepting others

7. Expresses and demonstrates appropriate perspective on a variety of problems

Personal Presentation (PP) Skills

1. Stays within own personal space appropriately

2. Shows appropriate body language while listening

3. Reads the body language of others

4. Expresses positive body language when communicating

5. Acknowledges and responds to others

6. Attempts to blend in with others

7. Independent with appropriate and positive personal presentation: grooming, hygiene, dress

8. Uses positive word choices (kind talk, positive self-talk, polite talk, encouragement, compliments, tact, appropriate talk for time/place/person)

9. Demonstrates flexibility when unexpected things happen

10. Communicates positively to problem-solve with others

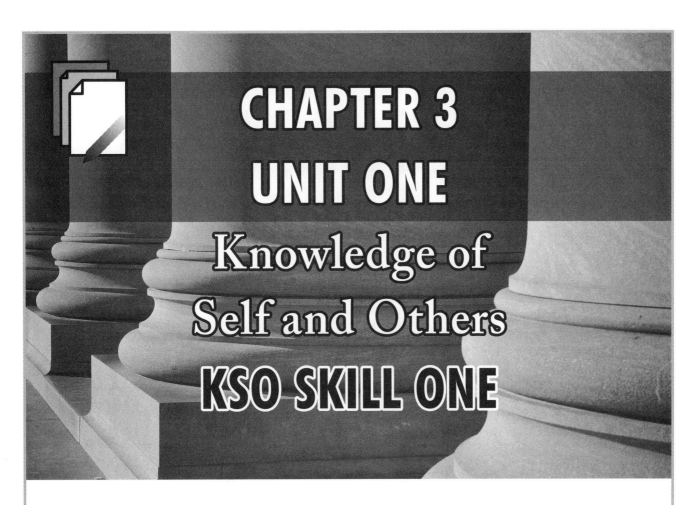

CHAPTER 3
UNIT ONE
Knowledge of Self and Others
KSO SKILL ONE

Positively expresses own personal preferences and opinions

SKILL INTRODUCTION:

Like everyone else, you have things you like and things you don't like! When you know what you like best then you can say and do things that are right for you. Everyone likes and doesn't like different things. It's not wrong or right to prefer something, or to not prefer something, or to have different opinions from other people. Other people should respect the way you feel, and it's okay for you to like or think something different than other people do. If you talk about what you like and think in a positive way, then you are showing respect for yourself and others.

Preferences (things you like) and opinions (what you think) are usually not "good" or "bad." Everyone is on the continuum line somewhere and no place on the line is good or bad, it's just who you are. You may enjoy both and are in the middle! It's fine to express an opinion as long as it is polite and if you do it at the right time and place, with the right people. Let's find out where you are on the line for some things! Point to the line or make a mark where you are.

CONTINUUM OF PREFERENCES AND OPINIONS

Do you prefer...

To play outside?	To play inside?

To eat sweet food?	To eat salty food?

Cool weather?	Hot weather?

To play alone?	With a friend?

To play sports?	To play video games?

Dogs?	Cats?

To do math?

Yes	No

To swim?

Yes	No

To read?

Yes	No

To try new foods?

Yes   No

To ride roller coasters?

Yes   No

To draw?

Yes   No

Do you tend to worry?

Not too much   A lot

Do you enjoy ...

Talking to people   Being quiet

Do you prefer ...

One or two friends   Lots of friends

Do you learn best by ...

Listening   Doing (hands on)

Do you prefer to work...

Alone   In a group

On a blank paper, make up your own preferences and opinions. You can place the date near the marks and check back in the future to see if your preferences or opinions change over time.

Positivity is:

Respectful	Accepting	Pleasant
Upbeat	Friendly	Not negative
Helpful	Interested	Not judging
Kind	Caring	Optimistic

What it looks like: Face is friendly and pleasant.

What it sounds like: Voice is not judging or negative, it is respectful and accepting.

How it makes others feel: Interested, they want to be your friend or stay your friend.

Let's practice!

My favorite animal is _____.

I don't like to eat _____.

I wish you would not make noise, it hurts my ears.

I like to play by myself sometimes.

I really don't like to go to the _____.

I need to take a break now please.

❏ I sounded positive   ❏ I looked positive

☑ UNIT ONE CHECKOUT:

Complete this form to see how you did with this skill.

I can:

❏ Tell what the skill is.

❏ Tell why it's important.

❏ Show how to do it.

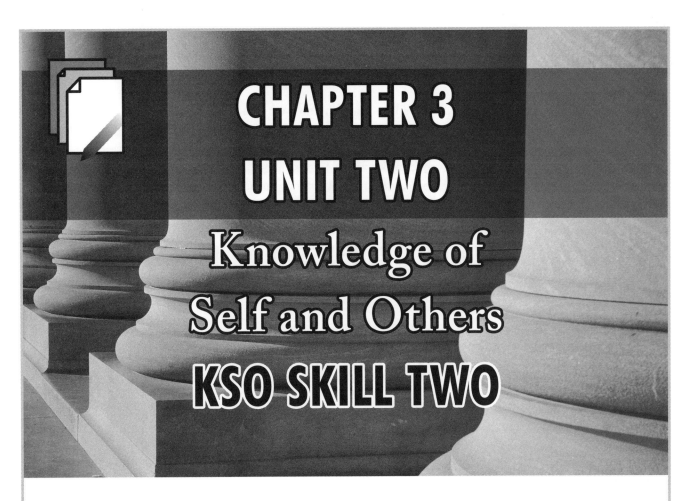

CHAPTER 3
UNIT TWO
Knowledge of Self and Others
KSO SKILL TWO

Positively expresses own strengths and weaknesses

SKILL INTRODUCTION:

Like everyone, you have things you are good at (strengths) and things you are not so good at (weaknesses). That's normal! Weaknesses are not bad, everyone has them and they are different for everyone. Even if something is not a strength for you, you can improve on it! Everyone can improve on their weaknesses. You have to be patient with your weaknesses, and not blame yourself or others. It is normal to need to improve, so you need to be okay with that. Parents, teachers, and bosses sometimes show you where you need to improve—that is their job. Listen carefully and patiently and try to make the changes so that you can do better. Everyone needs to make changes and improve sometimes. When you make a good change, then you can feel even better about all the good things that you do. It doesn't matter where you start on the line, the most important thing is that you are moving in the right direction, from weaker to stronger. When you move on the line, it shows you are improving! If you talk about your strengths and weaknesses in a positive way, then you are showing respect for yourself and others.

We all have strengths and weaknesses. It's important to know what our strengths and weaknesses are so that we know the things that we are good at and the things we may need help with and need to work on. Notice this line has an arrow at one end. That's because it doesn't matter where you start on this line, only that you know you can improve and move in the direction of strength. Let's find out where you are on the line for some things! Consider the list of "hard" and "soft" strengths below and point to the line or make a mark where you are for each.

CONTINUUM OF STRENGTHS AND WEAKNESSES

Weakness   Strength

STRENGTHS CHART

Examples of Hard Strengths:	Examples of Soft Strengths:
Math	Kind
Science	Helpful
History	Honest
Video games	Friendly
Building (e.g. blocks)	Positive
Reading	Caring
Drawing/art	Thoughtful
Writing	Patient
Cooking	Respectful
Household chores	Sharing
Outside chores	Hardworking
Driving	Cooperative
Sports	Responsible
Good grades	Organized
	Careful

Do you see how the soft strengths are different than the hard strengths? In many ways, they are more important than the hard strengths! Soft strengths will make a difference in your whole life and future, so they are the most important kinds of things to be good at. They are the strengths that will help you have friends, get along with others, and someday get and keep a job!

Positivity is:

Respectful	Accepting	Pleasant
Upbeat	Friendly	Not negative
Helpful	Interested	Not judging
Kind	Caring	Optimistic

What it looks like: Face is friendly and pleasant.

What it sounds like: Voice is not judging or negative, it is respectful and accepting.

How it makes others feel: : Interested, they want to be your friend or stay your friend.

Let's practice!

I am very good at _____.

_____ is more of a weakness for me.

Sometimes I am not so good at _____, but I am working to improve.

❑ I sounded positive   ❑ I looked positive

☑ UNIT TWO CHECKOUT:
Complete this form to see how you did with this skill.

I can:

❑ Tell what the skill is.

❑ Tell why it's important.

❑ Show how to do it.

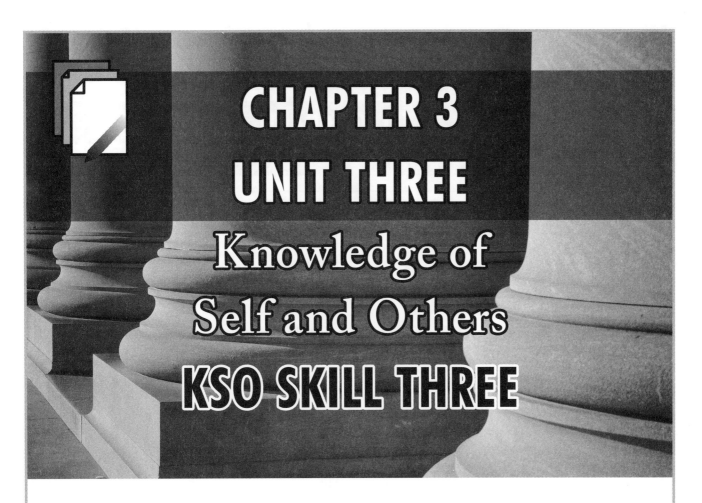

CHAPTER 3
UNIT THREE
Knowledge of
Self and Others
KSO SKILL THREE

Accurately expresses a variety of feeling words, both positive and negative, for own feelings and those of others.

SKILL INTRODUCTION:

Everyone has feelings. Feelings are not good or bad, they are just *comfortable* or *uncomfortable*. Sometimes it is hard to know which feeling you are having. You might think you are angry, when really there is another feeling that better describes how you are feeling. For example, maybe you think you feel angry when you get a bad grade, when really you are feeling disappointed and frustrated. It's important to describe your feelings as accurately as you can. You also must try to figure out just exactly how other people are feeling, so you can say and do the appropriate and best thing. They might have a totally different feeling about something than you do, so you have to be careful that what you say is respectful and positive! All feelings are okay, whether they are the same or different than yours. When you accurately talk about your feelings and the feelings of other people, you are respectful and you can solve problems and get along better with others.

FEELINGS CHART

Examples of Comfortable Feelings:	Examples of Uncomfortable Feelings:
Happy	Sad
Excited	Frustrated
Confident	Embarrassed
Proud	Disappointed
Pleased	Nervous
Calm	Anxious
Peaceful	Scared
Joyful	Furious
Respected	Annoyed
Silly	Irritable (grouchy)
Awesome	Worried
Loved	Tired
Cheerful	Hungry
Energetic	Hurt
Determined	Hopeless
Hopeful	Lonely
Surprised	Overwhelmed
Upbeat	

INTENSITY LEVEL FOR FEELINGS

0 = Not at all	1 = A little	2 = Somewhat	3 = Quite a bit	4 = Very

Choose a feeling word from the feelings chart for each scenario. Then choose a number from the scale below to describe the intensity of that feeling.

How do you feel when it's your birthday?

When you lose at a game?

When you don't get to do something you were looking forward to?

About presenting to the class?

Before you take a test?

Now ask someone else how they feel in these situations and what number describes the intensity of his or her feelings. Notice how you may have the same feeling as someone else, but a different number for intensity. We all feel things a bit differently and that's okay.

It is very important to identify and express your feelings accurately. Sometimes we think we are angry, when really there is another feeling word that would better describe how we are feeling. For example, maybe you expressed anger when you got a bad grade, but really you felt disappointed and frustrated. Maybe you expressed anger that you had to give a presentation in front of the class when you really felt anxious and nervous. Understanding how you're really feeling and expressing it accurately can help you deal with uncomfortable feelings and solve problems.

Think about a time you felt angry, then consider what other feelings you may have been feeling in that situation.

Below are some examples of situations that someone may react to with anger, when maybe it is really another feeling! Think of another feeling (besides angry/mad or furious) for each situation.

FEELINGS CHART

Examples of Uncomfortable Feelings:

Sad	Annoyed
Frustrated	Irritable (grouchy)
Embarrassed	Worried
Disappointed	Tired
Nervous	Hungry
Anxious	Hurt
Angry	Hopeless
Scared	Lonely
Furious	Overwhelmed

- You drop your tray in the cafeteria and everyone laughs.

- You don't get the present you wanted for your birthday.

- You have to wait an extra week to go see a movie you've been looking forward to.

- You can't finish what you are doing (building something, playing a game) and have to leave for an appointment.

- You have a dentist appointment and you strongly dislike going to the dentist.

- You got a B instead of an A on a test in school.

- You have to work with a group and you prefer to work alone.

- You forgot your lunch.

- Someone told you to "shut up" at school.

- Someone keeps poking you with their pencil.

- Your brother calls you names.

- Your favorite toy or game broke.

- Someone you love has a serious illness.

☑ UNIT TWO CHECKOUT:

Complete this form to see how you did with this skill.

I can:

❑ Tell what the skill is.

❑ Tell why it's important.

❑ Show how to do it.

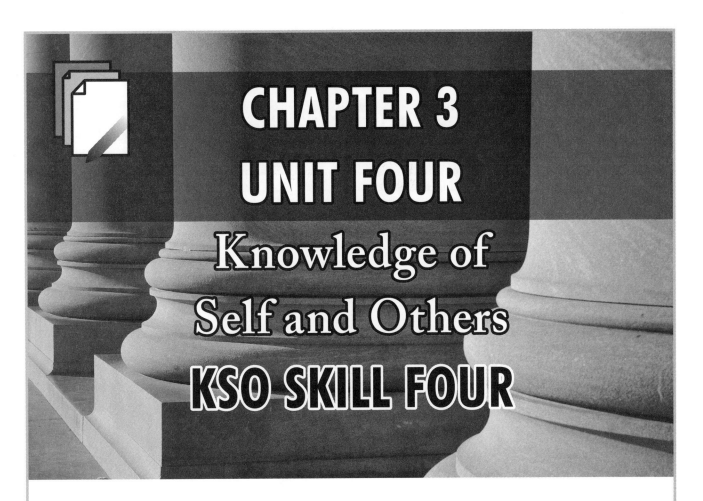

CHAPTER 3
UNIT FOUR
Knowledge of Self and Others
KSO SKILL FOUR

Accurately describes and positively frames ASD

SKILL INTRODUCTION:

Many people have conditions that make some things harder to do, and have to practice and improve so they can do what they want to. Autism spectrum disorder makes some things harder for you. But it also makes you unique and special! ASD is not the most important thing or the biggest thing to know about you—you are a lot more than that! Your family, friends, and teachers value you for who you are and will help you with anything that ASD makes hard for you. You can improve on weaker areas and make them stronger. If you can talk about having ASD in a positive way, then you show respect for yourself and help other people understand you, respect you, help you if you need it, and be your friend.

STRENGTHS CHART

Examples of Hard Strengths:	Examples of Soft Strengths:
Math	Kind
Science	Helpful
History	Honest
Video games	Friendly
Puzzles	Positive
Building (e.g. blocks)	Caring
Reading	Thoughtful
Drawing/art	Patient
Writing	Respectful
Cooking	Sharing
Household chores	Hardworking
Outside chores	Cooperative
Driving	Responsible
Sports	Organized
Good grades	Careful

CONTINUUM OF STRENGTHS AND WEAKNESSES

Weakness ⟶ Strength

These are my strengths:

What makes me most special is: _____

_____.

(Parent) What makes my son/daughter most special is: _____

_____.

FEELINGS CHART

Examples of Comfortable Feelings:	Examples of Uncomfortable Feelings:
Happy	Sad
Excited	Frustrated
Confident	Embarrassed
Proud	Disappointed
Pleased	Nervous
Calm	Anxious
Peaceful	Scared
Joyful	Furious
Respected	Annoyed
Silly	Irritable (grouchy)
Awesome	Worried
Loved	Tired
Cheerful	Hungry
Energetic	Hurt
Determined	Hopeless
Hopeful	Lonely
Surprised	Overwhelmed
Upbeat	

INTENSITY LEVEL FOR FEELINGS

0 = Not at all	1 = A little	2 = Somewhat	3 = Quite a bit	4 = Very

Overall my feeling about ASD is: _____

The intensity of this feeling for me is: _____

My comfortable feeling about having ASD is: _____

The intensity of this feeling for me is: _____

My uncomfortable feeling about having ASD is: _____

The intensity of this feeling for me is: _____

If you have a very uncomfortable feeling about having ASD, remember, it's normal to feel uncomfortable about something that can make things difficult for you. Everyone has strengths and weaknesses and everyone gets uncomfortable when things are difficult. That is a normal feeling to have. Although you may feel uncomfortable with having weaknesses, it is important to remember that everyone has weaknesses. Also remember all the strengths that you have and the things that make you special. They are *the most important things* about you!

☑ UNIT FOUR CHECKOUT:

Complete this form to see how you did with this skill.

I can:

❑ Tell what the skill is.

❑ Tell why it's important.

❑ Show how to do it.

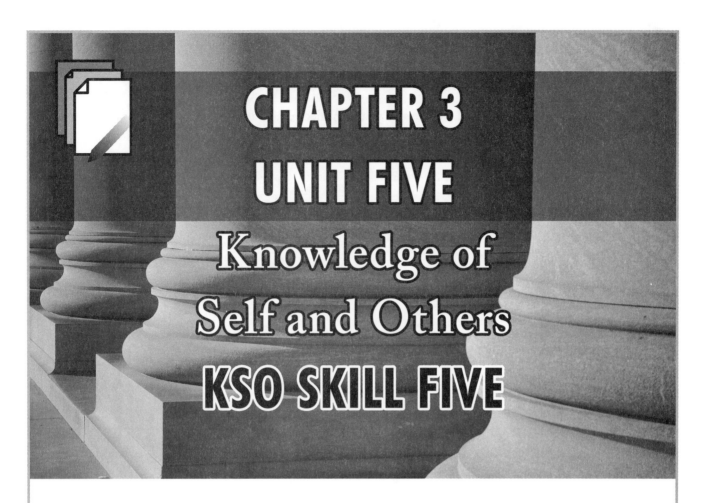

CHAPTER 3
UNIT FIVE
Knowledge of Self and Others
KSO SKILL FIVE

Expresses and demonstrates self-acceptance

SKILL INTRODUCTION:

Everyone has different strengths and weaknesses and those are not good or bad, they are just different! Even if something is not a strength for someone, he or she can improve on it. Everyone can improve on their weaknesses, that's why we talk about it and practice. ASD makes some things hard for you, but also makes you unique and special. With practice, you can improve the things that ASD makes hard for you. If you talk positively about your own strengths and weaknesses, you show respect for yourself and help other people understand you, respect you, help you if you need it, and be your friend.

Review some of the strengths and weaknesses you identified earlier and the things that make you most special. Now practice talking about your strengths and weaknesses in a positive way.

Positivity is:

Respectful	Accepting	Pleasant
Upbeat	Friendly	Not negative
Helpful	Interested	Not judging
Kind	Caring	Optimistic

What it looks like: Face is friendly and pleasant.

What it sounds like: Voice is upbeat, accepting.

How it makes others feel: Interested, they may want to know more about you.

Let's practice!

I'm not very good at _____,
but I'm awesome at _____.

_____ is better than me at _____, but I'm better
at _____.

Having ASD helps me to be strong at _____, but can make _____
_____ difficult.

Something I really like about myself is _____.

❏ I sounded positive   ❏ I looked positive

☑ UNIT FIVE CHECKOUT:

Complete this form to see how you did with this skill.

I can:

❏ Tell what the skill is.

❏ Tell why it's important.

❏ Show how to do it.

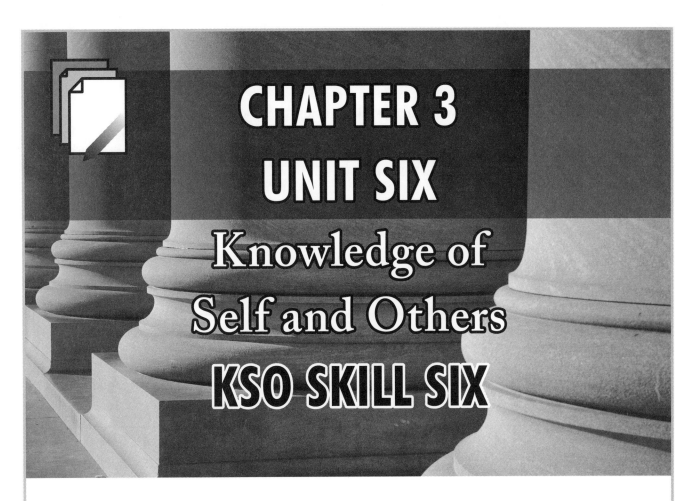

CHAPTER 3
UNIT SIX
Knowledge of Self and Others
KSO SKILL SIX

Expresses and demonstrates accepting others

SKILL INTRODUCTION:

Everyone is different! Everyone has different strengths and weaknesses, preferences, opinions, and feelings, just like you. Those are not good or bad, just different. Someone else might feel differently than you do about the same thing, and that is all right and perfectly normal. They will have different strengths and weaknesses than you, and think differently about things, but that's okay, too. Everyone is different, special, and deserves respect and kindness. When you are positive and respectful to others, even when they are different than you, that shows respect. When you respect others, it helps you to get along, make friends, and have a good reputation.

Let's pick someone you know very well (parent, sibling, grandparent, cousin, etc.) and figure out where they are on this line. What do they prefer? What are their opinions? If we are not sure, we can ask them. Then, let's compare it to what you preferred for each one of these. Remember, *there are no right or wrong answers,* and they might be in the middle. All answers are okay!

CONTINUUM OF PREFERENCES AND OPINIONS

_____ *prefers…*

To play outside?	To play inside?

To eat sweet food?	To eat salty food?

Cool weather?	Hot weather?

To play alone?	With a friend?

To play sports?	To play video games?

Dogs?	Cats?

To do math?

Yes	No

To swim?

Yes	No

To read?

Yes	No

To try new foods?

_____

Yes   No

To ride roller coasters?

_____

Yes   No

To draw?

_____

Yes   No

On another piece of paper, you may also make up other preferences and opinions and mark yourself on the line. Think about your special interest areas or strong opinions. Would the other people you know like those same things? Do they like them as much as you do?

Pick someone you know very well (parent, sibling, grandparent, cousin, etc.). Ask him/her to help you find out where he or she is on the continuum of strengths and weaknesses, for the strengths listed below. Compare these with your own strengths and weaknesses. They will be different, and that's good! Remember that we all have strengths and weakness, and we all can improve.

Who did I ask? _____

CONTINUUM OF STRENGTHS AND WEAKNESSES

Weakness   **Strength**

STRENGTHS CHART

Examples of Hard Strengths:		Examples of Soft Strengths:	
Math	Drawing/art	Kind	Patient
Science	Writing	Helpful	Respectful
History	Cooking	Honest	Sharing
Video games	Household chores	Friendly	Hardworking
Puzzles	Outside chores	Positive	Cooperative
Building (e.g. blocks)	Driving	Caring	Responsible
Reading	Sports	Thoughtful	Organized

Positivity is:

Respectful	Accepting	Pleasant
Upbeat	Friendly	Not negative
Helpful	Interested	Not judging
Kind	Caring	Optimistic

What it looks like: Face is friendly and pleasant.

What it sounds like: Voice is not judging or negative, it is respectful and accepting.

How it makes others feel: Respected, they want to be your friend or stay your friend.

Let's practice!

_____ really likes _____. That's okay!

I don't like _____, but _____ does.

_____ likes to eat _____ (something I don't like).

_____ doesn't like _____ (something I love).

THE COMMENTING RULE:

Remember to ask yourself, before talking about something that someone is NOT good at, is it nice and is it necessary to talk about it? If that person starts talking about it first, you might reply positively, as below:

I'm pretty good at _____, maybe I can help you?

_____ is not very good at _____, but he/she is really

good at _____.

I'm not very good at _____, but you are!

You are very good at _____!

It's okay that you're not very strong at _____, you can work on it!

❏ I sounded positive   ❏ I looked positive

Everyone has feelings. Sometimes people feel differently than we do about the very same thing. Pick something you feel strongly about (a four on the scale below). Then think of or find someone who only feels a zero, a one, or a two about that same thing. Now pick something else that you don't feel strongly about (a zero or one). Then think of or find someone who feels that feeling very strongly (a four) for that same thing.

INTENSITY LEVEL FOR FEELINGS

0 = Not at all	1 = A little	2 = Somewhat	3 = Quite a bit	4 = Very

Positivity is:

Respectful	Accepting	Pleasant
Upbeat	Friendly	Not negative
Helpful	Interested	Not judging
Kind	Caring	Optimistic

What it looks like: Face is friendly and pleasant.

What it sounds like: Voice is not judging or negative, it is respectful and accepting.

How it makes others feel: Respected, they want to be your friend or stay your friend.

Let's practice!

I feel very _____ when _____.

_____ doesn't feel _____ at all about this and that's okay.

I don't mind _____, but _____ gets very

_____ about that. Even though I don't think it's a big deal, it is a big

deal to _____, and that's okay.

❑ I sounded positive   ❑ I looked positive

☑ UNIT SIX CHECKOUT:

Complete this form to see how you did with this skill.

I can:

❑ Tell what the skill is.

❑ Tell why it's important.

❑ Show how to do it.

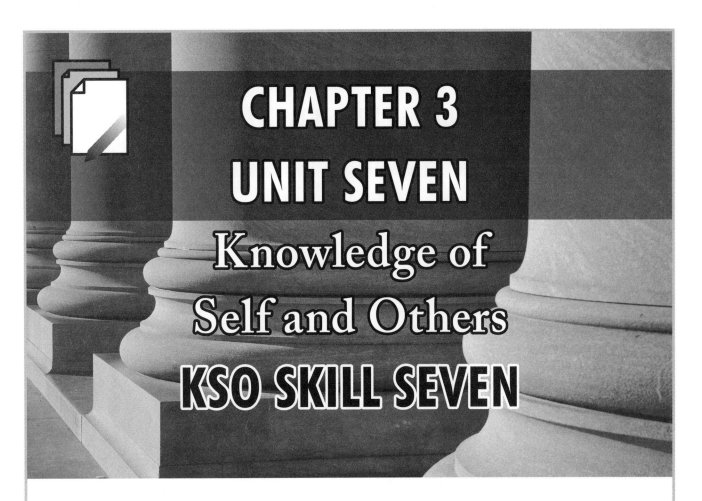

CHAPTER 3
UNIT SEVEN
Knowledge of Self and Others
KSO SKILL SEVEN

Expresses and demonstrates appropriate perspective on a variety of problems

SKILL INTRODUCTION:

It's important to know what kind of problem you are having so you can react appropriately and figure out how to solve it. Sometimes things are out of our control, sometimes it's just an accident or a mistake, and sometimes things are just difficult. Often, an uncomfortable feeling about a problem will feel like anger when you are really feeling frustrated, overwhelmed, jealous, hurt, or embarrassed. It is important to describe your feelings accurately and avoid blaming yourself or others. Everyone struggles with problems, and you are learning just like everyone else. Most problems are not anyone's fault, and everyone can improve and do better next time. Think about what kind of problem you are having, what kind of feeling you are really having, how strong your feeling is, and if that's appropriate for the kind of problem it is. Try to figure out how other people are feeling, too, so you can say and do the best thing in that situation. When you talk about a problem positively, you can get it solved, people will respect you, and you will have a good reputation.

PROBLEM PERSPECTIVE TOOL

When problems happen ... which kind of problem is it?

A. "Oh well, these things just happen!"

B. "That's okay, it was just an accident."

C. "It's just hard ..."

D. "Whoops, my mistake!"

E. "It was on purpose to hurt or bother me!"

Examples of problems:
- You drop your tray in the cafeteria and everyone laughs.
- You don't get the present you wanted for your birthday.
- You have to wait an extra week to go see a movie you've been looking forward to.
- You can't finish what you are doing (building something, playing a game) and have to leave for an appointment.
- You have a dentist appointment and you strongly dislike going to the dentist.
- You got a B instead of an A on a test in school.
- You have to work with a group and you prefer to work alone.
- You forget your lunch.
- Someone tells you to "shut up" at school.
- Someone keeps poking you with their pencil.
- Your brother calls you names.
- Your favorite toy or game breaks.
- Someone you love has a serious illness.
- You have to ask someone for help when you got lost.

For each of the above:

A. **What kind of problem is it (A, B, C, D, or E) ?**

B. **What's the feeling you have?**
   Check out the feelings chart below for the word that describes it best. Notice that problems A through D are not on purpose to hurt or bother you, so you should not blame anyone for those. For problems that are not on purpose to hurt or bother you, use at least one feeling word in place of, or in addition to, "angry," "mad," or "furious."

FEELINGS CHART

Examples of Uncomfortable Feelings

Sad	Annoyed	Angry
Frustrated	Irritable (grouchy)	Hopeless
Embarrassed	Worried	Scared
Disappointed	Tired	Furious
Nervous	Hungry	Lonely
Anxious	Hurt	Overwhelmed

C. How strong is your feeling?

INTENSITY LEVEL FOR FEELINGS

0 = Not at all	1 = A little	2 = Somewhat	3 = Quite a bit	4 = Very

Discuss with your parent or other person

How appropriate is your feeling and the intensity of your feeling for the kind of problem it is? What does your parent think is the best feeling word for your situation? What is an appropriate intensity for this problem? Pick someone that you know very well. How would he or she feel about each of the problems? Is it different than you would feel?

It is important to remember that sometimes people feel very differently than we do about the very same thing. They may have different opinions and preferences about the same thing, too. That is normal and okay. It is important to know how other people are feeling or thinking about something, and to show respect for their opinions and emotions. A problem or an uncomfortable feeling for you might feel okay or not be a problem at all to someone else, or they might just be doing the best they can and your problem is no one's fault. When you have problems, it is important to remember that other people might feel differently about your problem, and their feelings and opinions need to be respected. Stay positive!

Positivity is:

Respectful	Accepting	Pleasant
Upbeat	Friendly	Not negative
Helpful	Interested	Not judging
Kind	Caring	Optimistic

What it looks like: Face is friendly and pleasant.

What it sounds like: Voice is not judging or negative, it is respectful and accepting.

How it makes others feel: Respected, they want to be your friend or stay your friend.

Let's practice!

Pretend you have the following problems. Think about how the other person might be feeling. Check the feelings chart at the bottom if you are not sure. Practice responding to your problem with positivity and respecting the other person's feelings.

Problem: You didn't get the present you wanted for your birthday, you got something else. It made you feel upset, but you know that sometimes these things just happen. (What is the gift giver feeling?)

Say this with positivity: "Thank you very much for this present."

Problem: You have to wait an extra week to go see a movie you've been looking forward to because Mom is too busy to take you now. This made you feel frustrated and disappointed, but you know that these things just happen sometimes. (What is Mom feeling?)

Say this with positivity: "It's okay, these things just happen. I know you are busy right now, it's not your fault."

Problem: Someone accidentally bumps into you hard and you drop all your books and almost fall down! You felt embarrassed, but you know it was just an accident. (What is the other person feeling?)

Say this with positivity: "That's okay. It was just an accident."

Problem: You got lost and had to ask someone for help to find your mom. It was embarrassing! (What is your helper feeling? What is Mom feeling?)

Say this with positivity: "Whoops, I guess I wasn't paying attention! Thank you for helping me."

❑ I sounded positive   ❑ I looked positive

FEELINGS

Examples of Comfortable Feelings		Examples of Uncomfortable Feelings	
Happy	Silly	Sad	Annoyed
Excited	Awesome	Frustrated	Irritable (grouchy)
Confident	Loved	Embarrassed	Worried
Proud	Cheerful	Disappointed	Tired
Pleased	Energetic	Nervous	Hungry
Calm	Determined	Anxious	Hurt
Peaceful	Hopeful	Angry	Hopeless
Joyful	Surprised	Scared	Lonely
Respected	Upbeat	Furious	Overwhelmed

☑ UNIT SEVEN CHECKOUT:

Complete this form to see how you did with this skill.

I can:

❑ Tell what the skill is.

❑ Tell why it's important.

❑ Show how to do it.

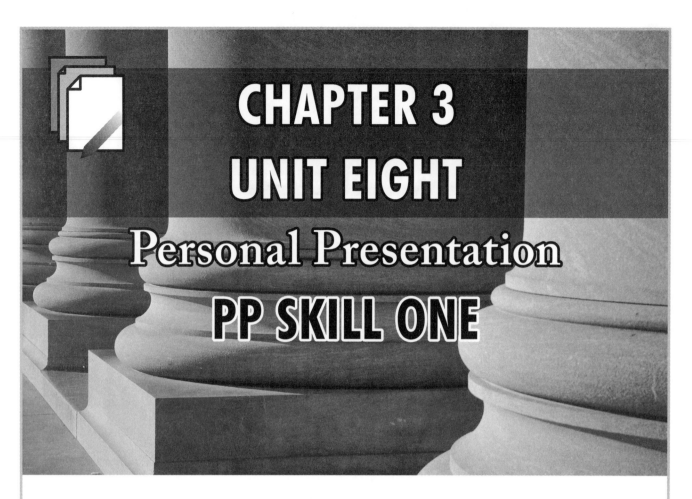

CHAPTER 3
UNIT EIGHT
Personal Presentation
PP SKILL ONE

Stays within own personal space appropriately

SKILL INTRODUCTION:

Everyone has a "bubble" area around them that is their own space. They usually don't like it if someone is inside that space with them. That is too close! It doesn't matter if you are talking to them or playing with them or just being in the same room with them—you need to stay in your own space (your own "bubble") and not come into theirs. It is often okay to be in someone's bubble if it is a family member or someone you know very well, but it is good to be careful with your body and your arms, hands, and legs, and to keep them in your own space almost all the time. Then everyone feels more comfortable, and people will like to be around you.

How do people feel when you are in their bubble/space? How do you feel when they are in yours? Note that these are uncomfortable feelings, unless it is a family member.

FEELINGS CHART

Examples of Uncomfortable Feelings:

Sad	Annoyed	Angry
Frustrated	Irritable (grouchy)	Hopeless
Embarrassed	Worried	Scared
Disappointed	Tired	Furious
Nervous	Hungry	Lonely
Anxious	Hurt	Overwhelmed
Bored	Ignored	Confused

INTENSITY LEVEL FOR FEELINGS

0 = Not at all	1 = A little	2 = Somewhat	3 = Quite a bit	4 = Very

POSITIVITY TOOL

Positivity is making others feel comfortable!

What it looks like: Body (including hands, arms, and legs) is within my own bubble.

How it makes others feel: : Comfortable, they want to be your friend or stay your friend.

CONTINUUM OF STRENGTHS AND WEAKNESSES

Weakness → **Strength**

Mark where staying in your own space is for you. If it is not a strength, let's practice moving it that direction.

Let's practice!

Talk to someone standing up and stay in your own space.

Talk to someone sitting next to you and stay in your own space.

Watch TV or play a game with someone and stay in your own space.

Walk up to someone and say hello and stay in your own space.

☑ UNIT EIGHT CHECKOUT:

Complete this form to see how you did with this skill.

I can:

❏ Tell what the skill is.

❏ Tell why it's important.

❏ Show how to do it.

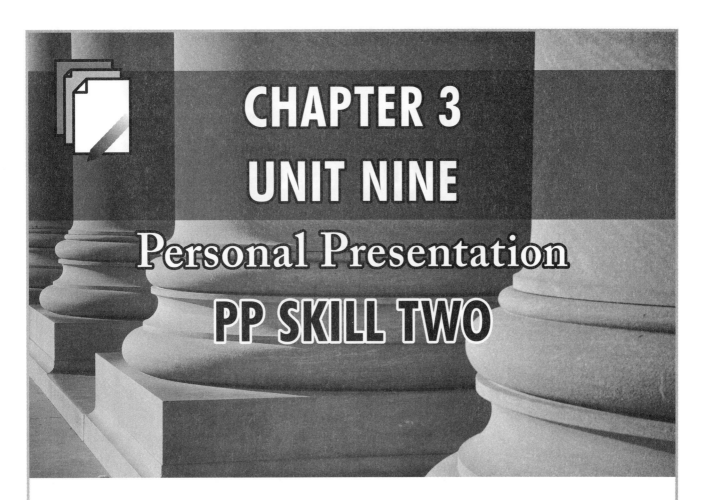

CHAPTER 3
UNIT NINE
Personal Presentation
PP SKILL TWO

Shows appropriate body language while listening

SKILL INTRODUCTION:

When other people talk, you listen. This shows that you respect them and that you are interested in what they are saying. How do you show with your body and your face that you are listening to someone? You sit upright, turn your shoulders to face them with your body, make eye contact, and have a friendly expression on your face. While you are listening, it is important to try to think about what people are saying and not think about other things. You don't talk until the other person stops talking. Good listening body language shows respect and interest in others.

How do people feel when you show good listening body language? How do they feel when you don't? How do you feel in both circumstances?

FEELINGS CHART

Examples of Comfortable Feelings:	Examples of Uncomfortable Feelings:
Happy	Sad
Excited	Frustrated
Confident	Embarrassed
Proud	Disappointed
Pleased	Nervous
Calm	Anxious
Peaceful	Angry
Joyful	Scared
Respected	Furious
Silly	Annoyed
Awesome	Irritable (grouchy)
Loved	Worried
Cheerful	Tired
Energetic	Hungry
Determined	Hurt
Hopeful	Hopeless
Surprised	Lonely
Upbeat	Overwhelmed
Interested	Bored
Important	Ignored

Parent: Demonstrate good listening body language while your child talks, and then demonstrate not using it. Let him or her try to show you good listening body language while you talk, making sure he/she understands all the elements of it: shoulders and face turned toward the speaker, eye contact, paying attention to what is being said, not interrupting, and pleasant and interested facial expression.

Talk about why showing good listening body language is important. Talk about the two "R's," respect and reputation, and how showing good listening body language makes people feel respected and helps give someone a good reputation.

Positivity is:

Respectful	Accepting	Pleasant
Upbeat	Friendly	Not negative
Helpful	Interested	Not judging
Kind	Caring	Optimistic

What it looks like: Interested, respectful, pleasant. Body is upright, shoulders facing the speaker, there is good eye contact, and a friendly expression on your face. Arms and legs are not moving.

What it sounds like: Quiet, not interrupting the person talking.

How it makes others feel: Respected and encouraged, they feel you are interested in them, they want to stay or be your friend.

Let's practice!

Practice positive body language while listening when your parent is talking.

Practice positive body language while listening when another family member is talking.

Practice positive body language while listening when someone outside the family is talking.

❑ I sounded positive   ❑ I looked positive

☑ UNIT NINE CHECKOUT:

Complete this form to see how you did with this skill.

I can:

❑ Tell what the skill is.

❑ Tell why it's important.

❑ Show how to do it.

CHAPTER 3
UNIT TEN
Personal Presentation
PP SKILL THREE

Reads the body language of others

SKILL INTRODUCTION:

People communicate with us using words, but they also send messages with their face, body, and voice tone. Sometimes someone says one thing with his words, but his body, face, and voice tone are sending a completely different message. We have to look carefully at the bodies and faces of people and listen to their voice tones to know what they are really saying. It's important to be sure, so that we can respond back to them appropriately. If you are not sure what someone really means, you should ask someone you can trust for help in figuring it out.

Parent: Say the following phrases to your child using either positive or negative body language. Ask your child to guess whether you are being positive or negative by looking at your body, face and listening carefully to your voice tone. Do you really mean what your words say?

"Good game"	"That looks great"	"No thank you"
"I'm sorry"	"I need help"	"Nice shoes"
"Good job"	"Thanks"	"I bet you did"

Reading body language helps us to know whether people are being kind and respectful. Think about the phrases that you just heard that had negative body language and voice tone. Using the feeling chart below, think about how you feel when someone speaks to you using negative body language. Also, try to guess how someone using negative body language might be feeling.

FEELINGS CHART

Examples of Uncomfortable Feelings:

Sad	Annoyed	Angry
Frustrated	Irritable (grouchy)	Hopeless
Embarrassed	Worried	Scared
Disappointed	Tired	Furious
Nervous	Hungry	Lonely
Anxious	Hurt	Overwhelmed
Bored	Ignored	Confused

Parent: Think of teachable moments! Change your body language so that it does not match with your words and see if your child can spot the disconnect. Use body language instead of words to see if she can figure out what you are communicating. Point out ambiguous messages with body language and words. Watch TV programs together and have your son or daughter tell you if the body language looks positive or negative, why they think that, and what people are *really* saying.

☑ UNIT TEN CHECKOUT:

Complete this form to see how you did with this skill.

I can:

❑ Tell what the skill is.

❑ Tell why it's important.

❑ Show how to do it.

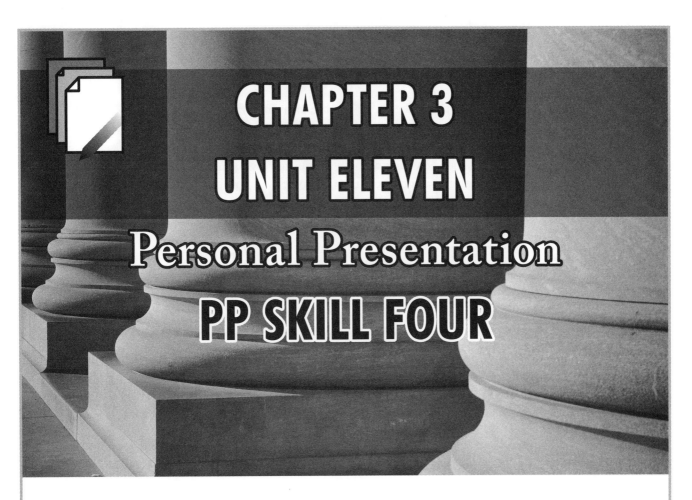

CHAPTER 3
UNIT ELEVEN
Personal Presentation
PP SKILL FOUR

Expresses positive body language when communicating

SKILL INTRODUCTION:

You use words to communicate but you also communicate with your body, face, and voice tone at the same time. When you speak to someone, make eye contact to show you are interested in what they are saying. Sit or stand upright with your body facing them and a pleasant, friendly facial expression. It is important for your voice to sound pleasant when you are speaking. If you use a calm and friendly voice, then people will want to listen to what you say and want to be around you. You should avoid using an angry, frustrated, loud, or bossy voice when you are speaking, even if you are upset. You must use a calm voice to ask for a break or to get help if you have a problem. People want to help you when your voice is calm and pleasant and your body language is positive. Positive body language helps others feel comfortable interacting with you and shows respect for others. It also helps you to make and keep friends.

If the body, face, and voice are negative, does it change the meaning of what you're communicating? How so? If you say "it's nice to see you" with a mean, grumpy, bored, or angry voice tone and face, what will the person listening to you think? Will he or she think you really are glad to see them? Practice saying the following phrases with positive and then negative body language. Try to change your voice tone and facial expression from friendly and calm to angry, bored, or grumpy. Can you hear the difference? Practice in front of a mirror; can you see the difference? Practice saying them to a family member. Can they see and hear the difference?

"Good game"	"That looks great"	"No thank you"
"I'm sorry"	"I need help"	"Nice shoes"
"Good job"	"Thanks"	"I bet you did"

How do other people feel when we use positive body language while we are talking to them? How do you feel? How do they feel if our body language is negative? Why is it important? Remember to consider respect and reputation.

FEELINGS CHART

Examples of Comfortable Feelings:	Examples of Uncomfortable Feelings:
Happy	Sad
Excited	Frustrated
Confident	Embarrassed
Proud	Disappointed
Pleased	Nervous
Calm	Anxious
Peaceful	Angry
Joyful	Scared
Respected	Furious
Silly	Annoyed
Awesome	Irritable (grouchy)
Loved	Worried
Cheerful	Tired
Energetic	Hungry
Determined	Hurt
Hopeful	Hopeless
Surprised	Lonely
Upbeat	Overwhelmed
Interested	Bored
Important	Ignored

INTENSITY LEVEL FOR FEELINGS

| 0 = Not at all | 1 = A little | 2 = Somewhat | 3 = Quite a bit | 4 = Very |

Think about people or kids that you know. Can you think of someone nice? Someone you think is mean? How do you know if they are nice or mean?

People notice others' behavior and form a judgement or opinion about them. Maybe you know someone who is fun to be around, or someone who complains a lot and is *not* fun to be around. Our behavior leads people to form an opinion or judgement about us and after a period of time, this can become our reputation. Consider the continuum line below. Where do you think others who are watching you or talking to you might think you are on this line? Is it true? Why or why not?

What kind of body language, including your facial expression and voice tone, could make others think you are mean, negative, angry, or difficult to get along with? What kind of body language could make others think you are kind, positive, happy, and easy to get along with?

Why is it important for others to see us as kind and positive rather than mean and negative? (Think of friendships, opportunities, respect, and reputation.)

Kind   Mean

Positive   Negative

Happy   Angry

Easy to get along with   Difficult to get along with

Positivity is:

Respectful	Accepting	Pleasant
Upbeat	Friendly	Not negative
Helpful	Interested	Not judging
Kind	Caring	Optimistic

What it looks like: Body language is positive, face is friendly, respectful.

What it sounds like: Voice is calm, kind, respectful.

How it makes others feel: Comfortable and respected, they want to be your friend or stay your friend.

Even if you need to say something that is negative, you can still make sure that you sound and look respectful and positive!

Let's practice!

"Please be quiet"   "I don't like those"
"This is really hard"   "It's not my favorite"
"No, thank you"   "That's disappointing"
"I don't want one"   "I wish I didn't have to go"

❑ I sounded positive   ❑ I looked positive

☑ UNIT ELEVEN CHECKOUT:

Complete this form to see how you did with this skill.

I can:

❑ Tell what the skill is.

❑ Tell why it's important.

❑ Show how to do it.

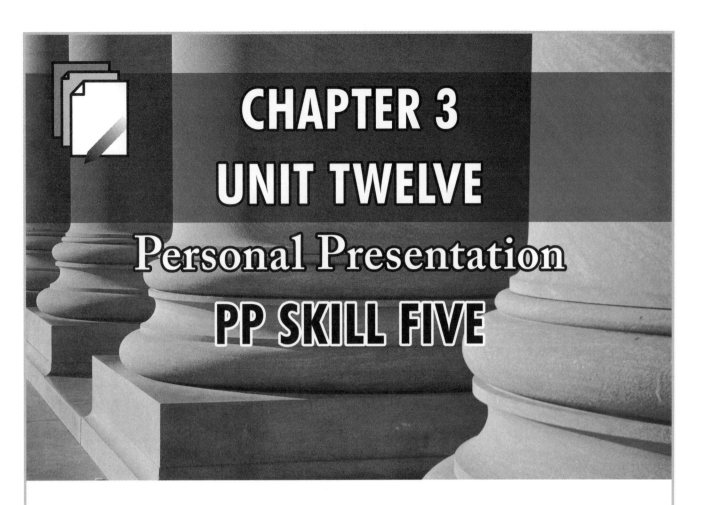

CHAPTER 3
UNIT TWELVE
Personal Presentation
PP SKILL FIVE

Acknowledges and responds to others

SKILL INTRODUCTION:

Whenever someone speaks to you, you should say something back. Even if someone just smiles, nods, or waves, you should do it back to them. Everyone likes to be noticed! If someone is talking about something, you can say something about that same thing, too, to show you are listening. If they ask you a question, you should answer it (if you know the answer). If you don't know the answer then you can say, "I don't know." If you are confused you can say, "I don't understand." It is okay to say "I don't know" or "I don't understand," but you should always say something back if someone speaks to you. Responding is polite and respectful, and people will want to talk to you or notice you if you always respond to them. This also helps you to have a good reputation.

How does someone feel when you respond back to them? Think about the following situations and tell how the other person might be feeling. Look at the feelings chart to help you pick the right feeling.

1. Someone says hello to you, and you say hello back with a friendly face.

   How does that person feel?

2. Someone waves at you and smiles, and you look down while frowning.

   How does that person feel?

3. A teacher asks you a question, and you ignore her and keep looking at your paper because you don't know the answer.

   How does your teacher feel?

4. Someone tells you about something they like, and you say, "I like that, too!"

   How does that person feel?

FEELINGS CHART

Examples of Comfortable Feelings:	Examples of Uncomfortable Feelings:
Happy	Sad
Excited	Frustrated
Confident	Embarrassed
Proud	Disappointed
Pleased	Nervous
Calm	Anxious
Peaceful	Angry
Joyful	Scared
Respected	Furious
Silly	Annoyed
Awesome	Irritable (grouchy)
Loved	Worried
Cheerful	Tired
Energetic	Hungry
Determined	Hurt
Hopeful	Hopeless
Surprised	Lonely
Upbeat	Overwhelmed
Interested	Bored
Important	Ignored

POSITIVITY TOOL

Positivity is:

Respectful	Accepting	Pleasant
Upbeat	Friendly	Not negative
Helpful	Interested	Not judging
Kind	Caring	Optimistic

What it looks like: : Face is friendly, pleasant, and looks interested; eye contact with other person; positive body language.

What it sounds like: Voice sounds interested.

How it makes others feel: Respected, cared about, they feel you are interested in them, they want to be your friend or stay your friend

Let's practice!

Practice doing the following with parent or another person. Show what you should do/say.

Someone waves to you. *(What should you do?)*

Someone says "hi" to you. *(What should you do/say?)*

Someone says, "Can I help you?" *(What should you do/say?)*

Someone smiles and gives you a thumbs up. *(What should you do?)*

Someone tells you about their favorite game. *(What should you do/say?)*

❑ I sounded positive   ❑ I looked positive

☑ UNIT TWELVE CHECKOUT:

Complete this form to see how you did with this skill.

I can:

❑ Tell what the skill is.

❑ Tell why it's important.

❑ Show how to do it.

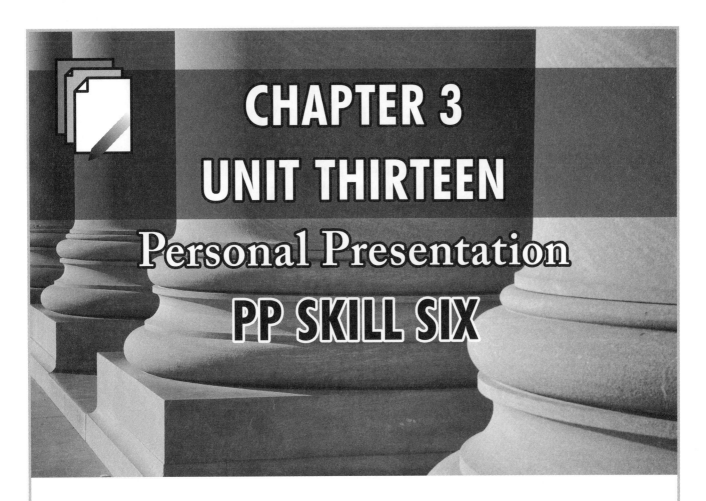

CHAPTER 3
UNIT THIRTEEN
Personal Presentation
PP SKILL SIX

Attempts to blend in with others

SKILL INTRODUCTION:

When you are in groups, you should look to see how other people are speaking and acting and try to match what they are doing. Other people notice how everyone else talks and acts—that's normal! They might decide things about you just by watching you. Are you kind? Are you quiet? Are you fun to be with? Do you seem like them, or different? If you are doing or saying things that others are not, this could be a problem. It is fine for you to "do your own thing" when you are at home or by yourself, but it is important to blend in when you are with others. When you blend with others it makes you more comfortable, helps you to look positive and like part of the group, and helps you gain friends and a good reputation.

BLENDING: LET'S MAKE IT STRONGER!

How well do you match with others? Look at the continuum line below. When you walk into a room, join a group, or play and hang out with others, can you blend in? Wherever you are on the line now, you can move it toward a strength! When you blend in with others, you are more comfortable and others see you are a good match for their group. When you walk into a group, check them out so you know how to match them.

CONTINUUM OF STRENGTHS AND WEAKNESSES

Weakness   **Strength**

Let's practice!

Sit like someone else is sitting.

Stand like someone else is standing.

Have the same facial expression as someone else.

Move like someone else.

Look the same direction someone else is looking.

Talk about the same things that others are talking about.

Think about it: does it match?

Everyone else is cleaning the banks of a pond, you pick up a large rock and toss it in the pond to make a big splash. *(Are you blending?)*

The other students are working in a group and you are checking out your favorite website on the computer. *(Are you blending?)*

All the students in the cafeteria are eating lunch and you are listening to music and dancing near your table. *(Are you blending?)*

Your class is looking at books in the library and you are, too. *(Are you blending?)*

Remember, if you are "doing your own thing" you are probably not blending in. People notice if you are doing something different and they might make a negative judgment about you. Go for positivity and blend!

POSITIVITY TOOL

Positivity is:

Respectful	Accepting	Pleasant
Upbeat	Friendly	Not negative
Helpful	Interested	Not judging
Kind	Caring	Optimistic

What it looks like: : Your face and body language are friendly and pleasant, focused and doing what others are doing, getting along with others, participating.

What it sounds like: Voice is not judging or negative. You are respectful, accepting, and talking about the same things others are talking about.

How it makes others feel: Comfortable, respected, they know what to expect from you and enjoy being with you, they want to be your friend or stay your friend.

Blending is matching others in a positive way!

Let's practice!

Blend with another person in your home for five minutes.

Blend with another person or group at school, church, or other place outside your home for five minutes.

Blend with someone you know very well.

Blend with someone you don't know very well.

❏ I sounded positive while blending   ❏ I looked positive while blending

☑ UNIT THIRTEEN CHECKOUT:

Complete this form to see how you did with this skill.

I can:

❏ Tell what the skill is.

❏ Tell why it's important.

❏ Show how to do it.

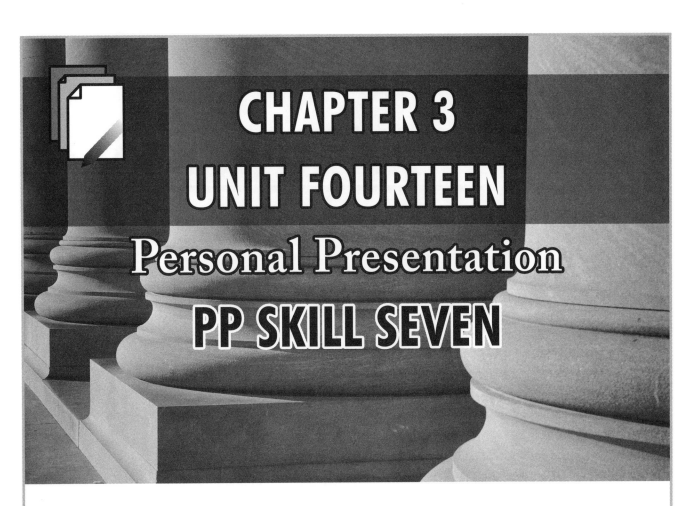

CHAPTER 3
UNIT FOURTEEN
Personal Presentation
PP SKILL SEVEN

Independent with appropriate and positive personal presentation: grooming, hygiene, dress

SKILL INTRODUCTION:

When you show up to school or work, you should think about what you look like. Other people will look at you and decide things about you from what they see. You want them to see positive things and make positive judgments about you, so it is important for you to be clean, neat, and appropriately dressed. These are called good hygiene, good grooming, and being well-dressed for the occasion. You should always check your reflection in the mirror before you leave to make sure that you look right. When other people look at you, they will know that you are ready to do your best work and to be friends. It is respectful to have good hygiene, grooming, and to be appropriately dressed, and it helps you to have a good reputation, too.

CONTINUUM OF STRENGTHS AND WEAKNESSES

Weakness   **Strength**

1. Look in a mirror. Find where you are on the line above for grooming.

Remember:

- Clothes should be clean, not wrinkled, and should match (don't forget matching socks!).

- Hair should be combed and teeth brushed.

- Fingernails should be trimmed.

- Did you groom yourself independently (without help) today?

2. Go make any improvements you need to make, then come back.

3. Look in the mirror again. Find where you are now on the continuum line above. Did you move toward "strength" for grooming?

4. Take a picture of yourself looking well-groomed and put it somewhere you can see it every day to remind you what you need to do to have good grooming daily.

POSITIVE PERSONAL PRESENTATION: HYGIENE

It is important to be clean, so you need to make sure that you wash your body and your hair every day. You need to use soap, shampoo, and deodorant so you smell good. You must wash your hands often and wear clean clothes. Other people will want to be around you when you are clean, and you will stay healthy, too.

CONTINUUM OF STRENGTHS AND WEAKNESSES

Weakness   **Strength**

1. Look in a mirror. Find where you are on the above line for hygiene. Ask yourself:

- Are you showered/bathed? Did you wash your whole body with soap?

   - Is your hair washed?

   - Did you put on deodorant?

   - Are your fingernails clean?

- Are your teeth brushed?

- Are your clothes clean?

- Did you clean yourself independently (without help) today?

2. Go make any improvements you need to make, then come back.

3. Look in the mirror again. Find where you are now on the continuum line above. Did you move toward "strength" for hygiene?

4. Take a picture of yourself looking clean and put it somewhere you can see it every day to remind you what you need to do to have good hygiene daily.

POSITIVE PERSONAL PRESENTATION: DRESS

You need to dress appropriately for the place you are going. Different clothes are for different activities. Some places are formal and you need to dress up, some places are informal and you can just wear clean, casual clothes. If you are not sure what is the appropriate thing to wear, you can ask a family member, a school staff person, or a friend. You can also look at what other people are wearing there and match them. It is respectful to dress appropriately for the place you are going, and it will help you to have a good reputation, too.

CONTINUUM OF STRENGTHS AND WEAKNESSES

Weakness   **Strength**

1. Look in a mirror. Find where you are on the line above for how you are dressed right now. Is it a weakness, a strength, or in the middle? Ask yourself:

   - Did I pick my clothes and get dressed by myself?

   - Are my clothes right for the weather?

   - Are my clothes right for what I am doing right now?

   - Are my clothes right for what I am planning to do next?

   - Are my clothes clean and without wrinkles?

   - Do my clothes match?

2. Go make any improvements you need to make, then come back.

3. Look in the mirror again. Find where you are now on the continuum line above. Did you move toward "strength" for dress?

4. Take a picture of yourself looking well-dressed and put it somewhere you can see it every day to remind you what you need to do to be well-dressed daily.

☑ UNIT FOURTEEN CHECKOUT:

Complete this form to see how you did with this skill.

I can:

❑ Tell what the skill is.

❑ Tell why it's important.

❑ Show how to do it.

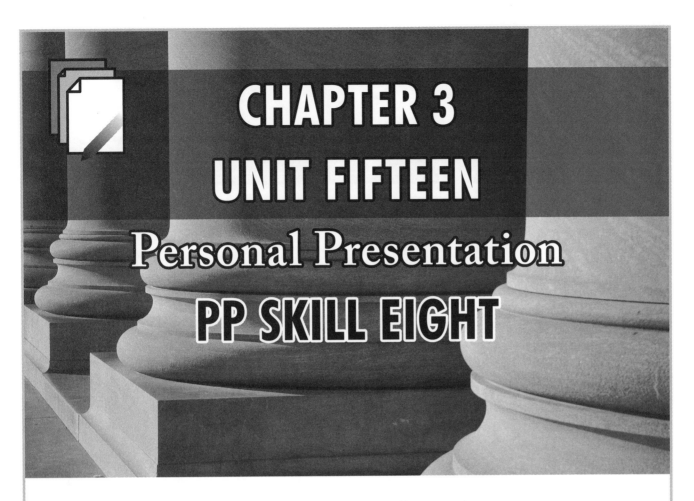

CHAPTER 3
UNIT FIFTEEN
Personal Presentation
PP SKILL EIGHT

Uses positive word choices (polite talk, kind talk, compliments, encouragement, positive self-talk, tact, appropriate talk for time/place/person)

SKILL INTRODUCTION:

Being positive with your words is very important. If you choose positive words when you speak to others, it helps you to build a positive reputation, shows respect, and helps you make friends. There are a lot of different positive word choices you can make! You can say polite and kind words to other people. You can say encouraging words to other people to help them stay positive when things are hard. You can also encourage yourself when things are hard, that is called "positive self-talk." Another positive word choice is compliments. It is important to pick the right time, place, and person to talk to. You should also say words that do not hurt anyone's feelings, that is called "tact." All these are positive word choices that help you show respect, make friends, and have a good reputation. Below are examples of positive word choices.

Polite Talk	Kind Talk	Compliments
"Please" "Thank you" "Excuse me" "I'm sorry"	"Are you okay?" "Can I help you?" "I'm sorry that happened" "Good game"	"You're good at math" "I like your drawing" "I like your shoes" "You're really nice"
Encouragement	**Positive Self-Talk**	**Tact**
"Nice job!" "Keep trying!" "You can do it!" "Good try!"	"I can do this" "Don't give up" "It's okay, these things happen" "I'll do better next time"	Think before you speak *Thinking:* This is so stupid. *Saying:* "This is kind of hard" or "I don't really like doing this" *Thinking:* "I don't want to sit with her" *Saying:* "I'm sorry, I can't today"

POLITE TALK

Speaking politely means saying "please," "thank you," "excuse me," and "I'm sorry." Often, adding "please" to a request can make a big difference in how it sounds to other people and their willingness to help. Speaking politely builds your reputation and makes other people feel respected.

Let's practice!

Consider the following scenarios and practice responding using polite word choices. You can use the suggestions or make up your own. Just remember to use a friendly face and pleasant voice tone!

Situation	What To Say
You need your teacher's help with an assignment.	"Can you please help me?"
You spilled your friend's milk at lunch and now she has nothing to drink.	"I'm sorry."
You bump into another student while putting on your coat.	"Excuse me."
You need a red marker and you notice another student is using one.	"Can I please use that marker when you're done?"
Your friend shares some cookies with you.	"Thank you."
You need to get in your locker and two students are standing in front of it talking.	"Excuse me, I need to open my locker."

Positivity is:

Respectful	Accepting	Pleasant
Upbeat	Friendly	Not negative
Helpful	Interested	Not judging
Kind	Caring	Optimistic

What it looks like: Face is friendly and pleasant.

What it sounds like: Voice is calm, kind, respectful, polite.

How it makes others feel: Comfortable and respected, they want to be your friend or stay your friend.

❑ I sounded positive   ❑ I looked positive

KIND TALK

Speaking kindly is a way to show other people you care. You speak kindly to your family and friends. You also speak kindly to people you don't know very well and even to people you may not like. Speaking kindly shows respect and builds your reputation as a kind, caring person.

Let's practice!

Think about the following situations. Practice saying something kind to the person in each situation. Remember to use positive body language!

Situation	What To Say
Your classmate fell down.	"Are you okay?"
Your mom can't find her car keys.	"Can I help you find them?"
Your brother's soccer team lost their game.	"Sorry you lost your game."
Your classmate just came back to school after being absent.	"It's nice to see you!"

Positivity is:

Respectful	Accepting	Pleasant
Upbeat	Friendly	Not negative
Helpful	Interested	Not judging
Kind	Caring	Optimistic

What it looks like: Face is friendly and pleasant, you look interested in the other person.

What it sounds like: Voice is calm, kind, respectful, and interested.

How it makes others feel: Comfortable and respected, they want to be your friend or stay your friend.

❑ I sounded positive ❑ I looked positive

COMPLIMENTS

You give someone a compliment when you notice something positive about him or her and say something nice about it. When you give someone a compliment, it shows that you are noticing that person and makes him or her feel important, happy, or proud. This is important because it builds your reputation as a kind, positive person who would be nice to know!

Let's practice!

Consider the following scenarios and practice responding by giving compliments. You can use the suggestions or make up your own, just remember to sound and look interested!

Situation	What To Say
You notice your classmate is wearing new shoes.	"I like your shoes!"
You notice your classmate's drawing.	"I like your drawing."
Your grandmother made cookies for your family.	"Your cookies are delicious!"
Your mom planted flowers in the front yard.	"The flowers look nice!"

Positivity is:

Respectful	Accepting	Pleasant
Upbeat	Friendly	Not negative
Helpful	Interested	Not judging
Kind	Caring	Optimistic

What it looks like: Face is friendly and pleasant, interested.

What it sounds like: Voice is kind, respectful, interested, enthusiastic.

How it makes others feel: : Comfortable and respected, they want to be your friend or stay your friend.

❑ I sounded positive   ❑ I looked positive

ENCOURAGEMENT

When someone else is feeling frustrated, sad, nervous, or scared, you might need to encourage him or her with positive word choices. You can say things like "good job," "nice try," "you can do it," or "that's okay" to make that person know you support him/her when something is hard. It is important to encourage others with positive words, even if they make a mistake. Encouragement can make someone feel hopeful and happy that you care. This will help you to make friends and have a good reputation.

Let's practice!

Consider the following scenarios and practice using encouragement. You can use the suggestions or make up your own, just remember to use a friendly face and upbeat tone of voice.

Situation	What To Say
You are watching your sister play soccer.	"You can do it!"
Your classmate got a bad grade on a test.	"It's okay, you'll do better next time."
Your little brother is learning to tie his shoes.	"Don't give up, you'll get it!"
Your classmate just gave her presentation in front of the class.	"Good job!"
Your classmate just gave the wrong answer.	"Good try."

Positivity is:

Respectful	Accepting	Pleasant
Upbeat	Friendly	Not negative
Helpful	Interested	Not judging
Kind	Caring	Optimistic

What it looks like: Face is friendly and pleasant, interested.

What it sounds like: Voice is upbeat, encouraging, interested.

How it makes others feel: Comfortable and respected, they want to be your friend or stay your friend.

❑ I sounded positive   ❑ I looked positive

POSITIVE SELF-TALK

It is important to speak positively to others to show respect and to have a good reputation. *It is also important to speak positively to yourself!* Positive self-talk is when you say something to encourage yourself. Sometimes things are difficult. You might feel frustrated or disappointed when something is difficult and might even want to give up. This is a normal feeling to have when something is hard. You can use positive self-talk to encourage yourself, to forgive yourself, or just to help you to feel better.

Let's practice!

Consider the following scenarios and practice using positive self-talk.

Situation	What To Say
You keep getting the wrong answer on your math paper.	"It's okay, I'll get it."
You are learning to play the guitar and keep making mistakes.	"It's okay to make mistakes, I'm just learning. I can do this."
You spill your milk.	"It's okay, these things happen, it was an accident."
You have to give a presentation in front of the class.	"I've got this, I can do it."
You volunteered to pass out papers but weren't chosen.	"It's okay, maybe I'll get to do it tomorrow."

Positivity is:

Respectful	Accepting	Pleasant
Upbeat	Friendly	Not negative
Helpful	Interested	Not judging
Kind	Caring	Optimistic

What it sounds like: Calm and accepting internal voice.

How it makes you feel: Calm, focused, able to solve problems and keep trying.

❏ I sounded positive   ❏ I looked positive

TACT

When you speak, you have to be careful to use words that do not hurt anyone's feelings or sound rude or bossy. This is called tact. You should use a pleasant tone of voice and use kind words when you speak. If you think of something that might sound rude or hurt someone's feelings, don't say it. Ask yourself, "Is it nice? Is it necessary?" before you say something to someone. That is "the commenting rule." If it is not nice to say, or not necessary to say, then you say nothing at all. When you are tactful, it helps you to make and keep friends, and gives you a good reputation.

Let's practice!

Consider the following situations and practice using tact. *Remember to use a pleasant face and voice tone.* Sometimes this is difficult when we are having a negative thought, but it is important to not hurt others' feelings.

Think	Say
You think the assignment is stupid.	"I don't really like doing this."
You don't want to sit with your classmate at lunch.	"I'm sorry, I can't today."
You think a game your classmate likes is boring.	"That game is okay, but I like this one better."
Your classmate offers you some of his lunch and you think it smells terrible.	"No thanks, I'm good with my lunch."
You think the hat your grandmother gave you is ugly.	"Thanks for the hat, I don't have one like this."
You think another student is not very smart.	Commenting rule: Is it nice? Is it necessary? Say nothing.

Positivity is:

Respectful	Accepting	Pleasant
Upbeat	Friendly	Not negative
Helpful	Interested	Not judging
Kind	Caring	Optimistic

What it looks like: Face is friendly and pleasant.

What it sounds like: Voice is pleasant, calm, kind, respectful.

How it makes others feel: Comfortable and respected, they want to be your friend or stay your friend.

☐ I sounded positive   ☐ I looked positive

PROBLEM PERSPECTIVE TOOL

When problems happen ... what can you say?
Look at the examples of positive word choices to help you think of what to say.

POSITIVE WORD CHOICES

Polite Talk	Kind Talk	Compliments
"Please" "Thank you" "Excuse me" "I'm sorry"	"Are you okay?" "Can I help you?" "I'm sorry that happened" "Good game"	"You're good at math" "I like your drawing" "I like your shoes" "You're really nice"
Encouragement	**Positive Self-Talk**	**Tact**
"Nice job!" "Keep trying!" "You can do it!" "Good try!"	"I can do this" "Don't give up" "It's okay, these things happen" "I'll do better next time"	Think before you speak Negative thought ➜ Positive words *Thinking:* "This is so stupid." *Saying:* "This is kind of hard" or "I don't really like doing this." *Thinking:* "I don't want to sit with her." *Saying:* "I'm sorry, I can't today." *Thinking:* "He's terrible at math." *Saying:* "It's okay, just keep trying."

A. **"Oh well, these things just happen!"**

- Your friend didn't get the game he wanted. Say something *encouraging*.

- Your new bike is hard to ride and you fall a lot. Say something *encouraging* to yourself.

- Mom was planning a picnic but then it rained. Mom worked hard to make the food! She is frustrated. Say something *encouraging* or *kind*.

- Your mom was supposed to get you cool new shoes but didn't have enough money, and she feels sad about that. Say something *kind* and *tactful*.

B. **"That's okay, it was just an accident."**

- Your friend spilled a drink on the floor at your house and is embarrassed. Say something *kind*.

- Your sister accidentally broke your puzzle and said she was sorry. She looks sad about it. Say something *kind*.

- You accidentally ran over the neighbor's flowers with your bike and they looked mad. Say something *polite*.

- You bumped into your brother and he spilled his milk. Say something *polite*.

C. **"It's just hard ..."**

- You found out that somebody's grandmother just died. Say something *kind*.

- You keep trying but you can't figure out the math problem. Ask for help *politely*.

- Your friend says he is bad at soccer. Say something *tactful*, *kind*, or *encouraging*.

- You can't get your locker open. Ask for help *politely* and *encourage yourself*.

D. **"Whoops, my mistake!"**

- You got a bad grade because you didn't study. Say something to *encourage yourself*.

- You broke the rules at school and got a detention. Say something to *encourage yourself*.

- You forgot to do your chores and Mom is mad at you. Say something *polite* to Mom, and something *encouraging to yourself*.

- You didn't follow directions and messed up something important. Say something *polite* to your parent, and something *encouraging to yourself*.

E. **"It was on purpose to hurt or bother me!"**

Someone at school keeps bothering you even though you told them to stop. Ask for help *politely*. Tell the right person (someone in charge), in the right place (privately if possible), at the right time (wait to speak to them when they are not speaking with someone else, or follow the process to make an appointment).

Tell what you would say, who you would say it to, when you would say it, and where you would say it:

_____

_____

_____

_____

_____

_____

_____

SPEAKING AT THE APPROPRIATE TIME, PLACE, AND TO THE APPROPRIATE PERSON

It is important to say the right thing at the right time, at the right place, and with the right person! You speak in different ways with different people: with friends you can speak in a more relaxed way; with adults and bosses, you speak more formally and respectfully. You must choose words that are polite and respectful with your friends, but especially with adults and bosses. It must be the right time to talk; it is important to be patient for your turn and to not to blurt words out when others are talking, or interrupt someone when they are busy. If you are talking about something private, you should share it only with the right people in a private place. If you communicate carefully then you are showing respect to others, and this helps friendships and your reputation with others.

Let's practice!

You have a problem with another student at school. You have tried to deal with it but it is still a problem. Do you:

A. Walk up to the teacher while he is teaching and tell him about it?

B. Shout it out while the teacher is speaking with students?

C. Wait until after class and ask the teacher if you can speak to him privately?

Practice saying these sentences looking and sounding *positive*:

"Mr. Martin, can I speak privately with you, please?"

"Mr. Martin, I need your help with something."

"I wonder if I can talk to you for a few minutes, Mr. Martin?"

Positivity is:

Respectful	Accepting	Pleasant
Upbeat	Friendly	Not negative
Helpful	Interested	Not judging
Kind	Caring	Optimistic

What it looks like: Face is friendly and pleasant, may look concerned if you have a problem.

What it sounds like: Voice is calm, respectful.

How it makes others feel: Interested in helping you with your issues, interested in hearing what you have to say, respectful of you.

❏ I sounded positive   ❏ I looked positive

PROBLEM PERSPECTIVE TOOL

When problems happen ... which kind of problem is it?

A. "Oh well, these things just happen!"

B. "That's okay, it was just an accident."

C. "It's just hard ..."

D. "Whoops, my mistake!"

E. "It was on purpose to hurt or bother me!"

There are some problems that you only talk about in private places, to trusted people, at the right time. These may be things about your body, your money, your family problems, your worries, or any uncomfortable feelings you have.

Parent: From more than one problem category above, brainstorm some personal situations with your child from that should only be shared in private places, with trusted people, at the right time.

For each of the above:

• Who is a trusted person to share this information with?

• Where is a private place to share this information with that person?

• When is an appropriate time to share this information?

• Practice exactly what to say for each situation you think of.

☑ UNIT FIFTEEN CHECKOUT:
Complete this form to see how you did with this skill.

I can:

❏ Tell what the skills are.

❏ Tell why they are important.

❏ Show how to do them.

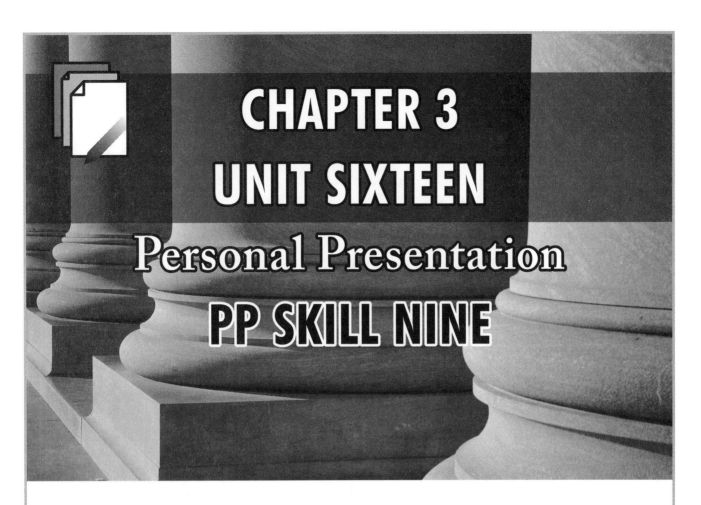

CHAPTER 3
UNIT SIXTEEN
Personal Presentation
PP SKILL NINE

Demonstrates flexibility when unexpected things happen

SKILL INTRODUCTION:

When unexpected things happen that make you change what you were planning, you have to stay flexible. This means that you use your own special ways to relax and feel less frustrated, then start again in a new way. Use a calm voice to ask for a break if you need it, or simply ask for help to do something in a new way. Sometimes, things happen that you don't expect; it's no one's fault, and you need to be flexible in these situations. When you are flexible, people know they can depend on you and they can work with you to solve problems. This helps you to have a good reputation with others.

Consider the scenarios below, the type of problem it is, and what would be a flexible thing to do in each instance. In parentheses is one suggestion. See if you can think of at least one other flexible thing you can do in each situation.

Parent: Point out to your child that each quoted statement is a positive way to view the problem and is something positive he or she can say when that kind of problem happens. Ask your child to practice saying it using positive body language for each situation.

PROBLEM PERSPECTIVE TOOL

When problems happen ... how do you show you are flexible?
Let's practice!

A. "Oh well, these things just happen!"

Situation	Flexible Solution
You planned to buy pizza for lunch but the menu was changed and they didn't have pizza.	Get something else for lunch.
Recess was changed from an "outdoor" recess to an "indoor" recess.	Think of something fun to do at indoor recess.
Your little sister got sick, so your mom can't take you to the movies as planned.	Pick out a movie to watch at home.
You like to stay home on Saturdays and play your favorite games. This Saturday you have to go to your grandparents' house to help them do yard work.	Help out at your grandparents and play your game later.
You like to sit in the seat by the door in science class. Your teacher needed to give that seat to another student in the class for private reasons.	Agree to move your seat.

B. "That's okay, it was just an accident."

Situation	Flexible Solution
Another student bumped into you in the cafeteria and your lunch fell on the floor.	Tell the lunch staff and ask for another lunch.
Your brother spilled water on your drawing.	Draw another picture.
You fell and ripped a hole in your favorite pants.	Choose a new favorite pair of pants.

C. "It's just hard ..."

Situation	Flexible Solution
You can't figure out the answer to the first problem on the test.	Skip that question and move on to the next one.
You are working on a project for school that needs pictures. Drawing is very difficult for you.	Cut out pictures from magazines instead.

D. "Whoops, my mistake!"

Situation	Flexible Solution
You dropped your wireless mouse and it broke.	Use a mouse with a wire until it can be replaced.
You forgot your favorite reading book at home and need a book to read at school.	Choose a different book to read.

E. **"It was on purpose to hurt or bother me!"**

Situation	Flexible Solution
Another student continues to call you "Joey" when your name is "James."	Send a clear message, telling him to please stop calling you by the wrong name. If he continues, you ask calmly to speak to a teacher or someone in the office.
Your brother's friend knows loud noises upset you but he turns their music up loud anyway.	Send a clear message, telling him to please play the music more quietly. Then if he continues it loudly, you ask your parent or other supervising adult to please make him stop and calmly explain why.

CONTINUUM OF STRENGTHS AND WEAKNESSES

Weakness   **Strength**

Are you flexible when unexpected things happen? Is it a strength for you? Does it need practice? Where are you on the line for the following situations? (If you answer "yes," you are flexible!)

YES   NO

Someone bumped your arm and made you miss a shot in a basketball game. Do you say, "It's okay, you didn't mean to bump my arm," and keep on playing?

YES   NO

You can't get your locker open and now you are late for class. Do you say to yourself, "It's okay, I will just tell them at the office that I need help and they will write me a pass," and solve the problem?

YES   NO

You tried out for the team and didn't make it. Do you say to yourself, "I will try out next year and maybe I will make it?"

YES   NO

You didn't get the game you wanted for your birthday, instead you got one that is just okay. Do you say "thank you" and play with the game you got?

YES   NO

POSITIVITY TOOL

Positivity is:

Respectful	Accepting	Pleasant
Upbeat	Friendly	Not negative
Helpful	Interested	Not judging
Kind	Caring	Optimistic

What it looks like: Face is friendly, calm, and pleasant. Positive body language.

What it sounds like: Voice is not judging or negative, is respectful, accepting, calm.

How it makes others feel: Respected, they feel they can depend on you, they want to be your friend or stay your friend.

Let's practice!

"Oh well, these things just happen!"

"That's okay, it is not your fault, it was just an accident."

"It's hard but I will keep trying"

"Whoops, that was my mistake. I will try harder next time."

❑ I sounded positive   ❑ I looked positive

☑ UNIT SIXTEEN CHECKOUT:

Complete this form to see how you did with this skill.

I can:

❑ Tell what the skill is.

❑ Tell why it's important.

❑ Show how to do it.

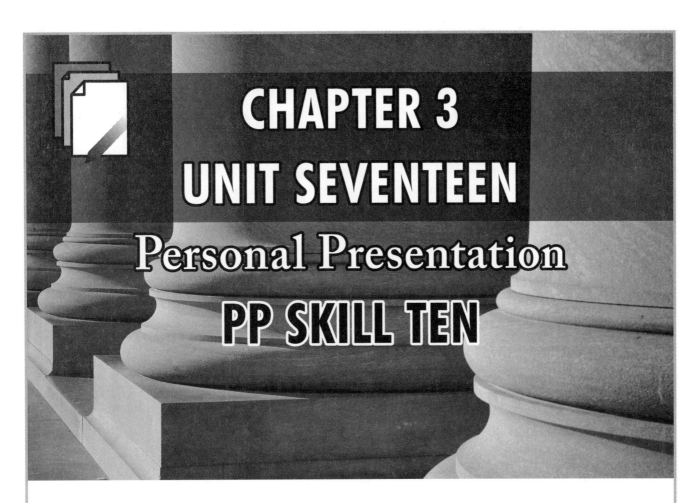

CHAPTER 3
UNIT SEVENTEEN
Personal Presentation
PP SKILL TEN

Communicates positively to problem-solve with others

SKILL INTRODUCTION:

When you have a problem, you have to figure out how to solve it. You can have a problem with a thing or a person, but we know that most problems are not on purpose so we don't blame anyone. You should try to fix the problem by talking to someone, this is called *communicating* to solve a problem. You will need to stay positive, patient, and calm while you communicate with someone about your problem. First, clearly explain what your problem is, then you will need to talk to and cooperate with someone else to find ways to solve your problem. It helps to solve problems if you communicate positively and work with others. It is not helpful to blame others or become frustrated. Stay positive! Your boss, teachers, friends, and family depend on you to communicate with them when you have a problem and to work patiently to solve it.

When problems happen . . . which kind of problem is it? When you know which kind of problem it is, then you will know how to communicate about it!

A. "Oh well, these things just happen!"

This kind of problem did not happen on purpose to hurt or bother you, and it is no one's fault. Sometimes things happen that we can't control, it is a part of life! Everyone experiences unwelcome surprises, setbacks, and changes. It is not appropriate to blame anyone for this kind of problem. Although you might feel frustrated, embarrassed, nervous, or some other uncomfortable feeling, it is not helpful and probably not appropriate to feel a "four" in intensity about this kind of problem. You need to think about the feelings of others as well as yourself and stay calm and patient. You may not need to communicate very much to deal with this kind of problem. *Positivity* in body language, including voice tone, is important. It is usually appropriate to say, "Oh well, these things just happen," and move on!

Communicate with others positively for this kind of problem!

What it looks like: Face is friendly and pleasant.

What it sounds like: Voice is not judging or negative, is respectful, accepting, calm.

How it makes others feel: Respected, they can depend on you to stay calm, they want to be your friend or stay your friend.

Let's practice!

Say these things with positivity—don't forget positive body language and voice tone!

"Oh well, these things just happen!"

"It's okay, we can do it another time."

"It's not your fault."

"Don't worry about it."

❑ I sounded positive   ❑ I looked positive

B. "That's okay, it was just an accident."

This kind of problem did not happen on purpose to hurt or bother you, and it is no one's fault. Sometimes things happen that are just accidents, it is a part of life! Accidents happen to everyone. It is not appropriate to blame anyone for this kind of problem. Although you might feel frustrated, embarrassed, nervous, or some other uncomfortable feeling, it is not helpful and probably not appropriate to feel a "four" in intensity for that feeling about this kind of problem. You need to think about the feelings of others as well as yourself and stay calm and patient. You may not need to communicate very much to deal with this kind of problem. *Positivity* in body language, including voice tone, is important. It is usually appropriate to say, "That's okay, it was just an accident," and move on!

Communicate with others positively for this kind of problem!

What it looks like: Face is friendly and pleasant.

What it sounds like: Voice is not judging or negative, is respectful, accepting, calm.

How it makes others feel: Respected, they can depend on you to stay calm, they want to be your friend or stay your friend.

Let's practice!

Say these things with positivity—don't forget positive body language and voice tone!

"That's okay, it was just an accident!"

"I'll be okay."

"I know you didn't mean to do it."

"Don't worry about it."

❑ I sounded positive   ❑ I looked positive

C. "It's just hard ..."

This kind of problem did not happen on purpose to hurt or bother you, and it is no one's fault. Sometimes things are just hard, it is a part of life! Everyone experiences things that are difficult. It is not appropriate to blame anyone for this kind of problem. You might feel frustrated, embarrassed, nervous, upset, or some other uncomfortable feeling, even up to a level "four" in intensity about a this kind of problem. You may need to communicate with someone to help you solve the problem and/or to help you with your feelings about the problem.

Look at the feelings intensity chart below. Remember that it is easier to communicate to solve a problem before you get to a "four," so don't wait!

INTENSITY LEVEL FOR FEELINGS

0 = Not at all	1 = A little	2 = Somewhat	3 = Quite a bit	4 = Very

Positivity is:

- Encouraging yourself
- Advocating for yourself
- Communicating calmly and clearly
- Communicating with positive word choices, including appropriate person/time/place and polite talk

Communicate with others positively for this kind of problem!

What it looks like: Face and all body language is friendly, pleasant, calm, patient.

What it sounds like: Voice is not judging or negative, is respectful, accepting, calm.

How it makes others feel: Respected, they can depend on you to stay calm, they want to help you, they want to be your friend or stay your friend.

Let's practice!

Say these things with positivity—don't forget positive body language and voice tone!

"Yeah, that thing is always hard for me."

"What do you think I should do?"

"Do you have any suggestions for what I can do about this?"

"Could you please help me with this?"

"I can do this if I just give myself more time."

❑ I sounded positive   ❑ I looked positive

D. "Whoops, my mistake!"

This kind of problem is your fault in some way, but making mistakes is a part of life! Everyone makes mistakes. When you make a mistake, you should forgive yourself and try to fix it or do better next time. You might feel frustrated, embarrassed, nervous, upset, or some other uncomfortable feeling, even at a "four" in intensity about this kind of problem. You may need to communicate with someone to help you solve the problem, fix the problem, avoid the problem in the future, and/or to help you with your feelings about the problem.

Look at the feelings intensity chart below. Remember that it is easier to communicate to solve a problem before you get to a "four," so don't wait!

INTENSITY LEVEL FOR FEELINGS

0 = Not at all	1 = A little	2 = Somewhat	3 = Quite a bit	4 = Very

Positivity is:

- Encouraging yourself

- Advocating for yourself

- Communicating calmly and clearly

- Communicating with positive word choices, including appropriate person/time/place and polite talk

What it looks like: Face and all body language is friendly, pleasant, calm, patient, accepting.

What it sounds like: Voice is not judging or negative, is respectful, accepting, calm, forgiving.

How it makes others feel: Respected, they can depend on you to stay calm, they want to help you, they want to be your friend or stay your friend.

Let's practice!

Say these things with positivity—don't forget positive body language and voice tone!

"I get really frustrated when I do that."

"I wish I hadn't done that!"

"Can you remind me about this? I keep making a mistake on it."

"I'm still a little mad at myself and I can't stop thinking about it. Can you help me with that?"

❏ I sounded positive   ❏ I looked positive

E. "It was on purpose to hurt or bother me!"

It is natural and understandable to be angry, frustrated, upset, sad, hurt, or embarrassed when someone does something on purpose to hurt or bother you. Review the intensity scale below. Remember that it is easier to communicate to solve a problem before you get to a "four," so don't wait! When someone does something on purpose to hurt or bother you, you need to communicate right away.

INTENSITY LEVEL FOR FEELINGS

0 = Not at all	1 = A little	2 = Somewhat	3 = Quite a bit	4 = Very

Positivity is:

- Encouraging yourself
- Advocating for yourself
- Communicating calmly and clearly
- Communicating with positive word choices, including appropriate person/time/place and polite talk

Let's practice!

Say these things with positivity—don't forget positive body language and voice tone!

1. Tell the person/people doing the behavior that you do not like it and they need to stop doing it.

   "I don't like it when you _____. I want you to stop."

2. If they don't stop, tell an adult or someone in charge. Ask them to help you with the problem.

   "Please help me make _____ stop doing _____.
   It makes me feel very _____."

❑ I communicated with positivity to solve my problem.

☑ UNIT SEVENTEEN CHECKOUT:
Complete this form to see how you did with this skill.

I can:

❑ Tell what the skill is.

❑ Tell why it's important.

❑ Show how to do it.

BASIC TOOLS

(not adapted for use with particular skills)

The seven tools are offered next in a basic format so that you, the parent, may utilize them in novel ways and adapt them to address real issues and problems that come up in your child's life (teachable moments!).

1 STRENGTHS CHART

Examples of Hard Strengths:	Examples of Soft Strengths:
Math	Kind
Science	Helpful
History	Honest
Video games	Friendly
Building (e.g. blocks)	Positive
Reading	Caring
Drawing/art	Thoughtful
Writing	Patient
Cooking	Respectful
Household chores	Sharing
Outside chores	Hardworking
Driving	Cooperative
Sports	Responsible
Good grades	Organized
	Careful

2 CONTINUUM OF STRENGTHS AND WEAKNESSES

Weakness   →   Strength

3 FEELINGS CHART

Examples of Comfortable Feelings:	Examples of Uncomfortable Feelings:
Happy	Sad
Excited	Frustrated
Confident	Embarrassed
Proud	Disappointed
Pleased	Nervous
Calm	Anxious
Peaceful	Angry
Joyful	Scared
Respected	Furious
Silly	Annoyed
Awesome	Irritable (grouchy)
Loved	Worried
Cheerful	Tired
Energetic	Hungry
Determined	Hurt
Hopeful	Hopeless
Surprised	Lonely
Upbeat	Overwhelmed
Interested	Bored
Important	Ignored

4 Do you prefer...

Option 1   OR   Option 2

5 INTENSITY LEVEL FOR FEELINGS

0 = Not at all	1 = A little	2 = Somewhat	3 = Quite a bit	4 = Very

6

Positivity is:

Respectful	Accepting	Pleasant
Upbeat	Friendly	Not negative
Helpful	Interested	Not judging
Kind	Caring	Optimistic

What it looks like: Face and body language is

What it sounds like: Voice tone is

How it makes others feel:

Let's practice!

❑ I sounded positive   ❑ I looked positive

7

PROBLEM PERSPECTIVE TOOL

When problems happen … which kind of problem is it?

A. "Oh well, these things just happen!"

B. "That's okay, it was just an accident."

C. "It's just hard …"

D. "Whoops, my mistake!"

E. "It was on purpose to hurt or bother me!"

CHAPTER 4
RAISING THE BAR: INCREASING THE SKILL ELEMENTS AND CARRYOVER

The culmination of foundational social-communication skills development at the highest level should translate to those soft skills detailed in Chapter Two, which have been shown to increase the chances of a young adult being successful vocationally. In this book, we have talked about prioritizing the development of the social-communication skills which support the requisite soft skills while raising your child with ASD. Because social-communication skills are particularly challenging for your child, the foundational skills will quite possibly need years of attention across many situations in life for all of the elements of each skill to become developed. While Chapter Three covered the basic elements of expressing knowledge of each of the skills, expressing understanding of their importance, and demonstrating them with your guidance, there are more elements that need to be covered for those social-communication skills to be achieved at the highest level. In this chapter, we will discuss the other elements for the skills and suggest ways that you can develop them.

The target elements of each skill include understanding what the skill is, knowing why it is important, expressing and demonstrating the skill with the right person/people, at the right time, in the right place/ situation, with an appropriate frequency, across contexts, and in coordination with other skills. Any of those elements may need guidance or help in the form of modeling, cues, and reminders, particularly early on and/or if the skill is very challenging for your child, but ultimately you are striving for a skill with all of the elements that is done independently. When a skill is done independently and with all of the necessary elements, this is called "carryover" or "generalization" of the skill. In this chapter, we will offer suggestions for increasing the number of skill "elements" that your child displays and working toward carryover, or independent use, of the skills.

In Chapter Three, you worked through all the skills with your child and created shared reference points while using visual tools. Your child should have achieved the following, for each of the skills:

1. Expressing understanding of the skill with help/guidance.
2. Expressing understanding of why the skill is important with help/guidance.
3. Demonstrating the skill with help (reminders, cues, models).

That is a good start! You now have a framework for referring back to the skills and building on them as situations arise in your child's life, as well as tools that you can use to reinforce the skills and extend them. Hopefully, your child has a positive outlook on further developing the skills and is engaged with you in addressing them. If you are having issues with the latter, please look for the suggestions on dealing with this in Chapter Three.

It is recommended that you pick one skill at a time to target and increase its elements. You may want to change your target skill weekly, depending on the response you get in terms of skill and interest by your child. It might work best to switch skills but target one particular element over several days or weeks; for example, focus on increasing the frequency of multiple skills such as blending, expressing and/or demonstrating acceptance, and using positive listening body language. This will target the same element (frequency) but change up the skills from one to the next with that focus.

Regarding which skill to choose to enhance with more elements, we would offer the following ideas to consider:

1. Pick a skill for which there are many natural opportunities to demonstrate or use it in your lives.

2. Pick a skill that you feel your child is interested in improving.

3. Pick a skill for which your child has a good grasp of the basics.

4. Pick a skill for which your child is showing some spontaneous use of the tools for the skill, or spontaneously refers to, etc.

5. Pick a skill that your child desperately needs to make some growth in and/or a skill that would be a big improvement in your lives if he or she were to make progress in.

6. Ask your child to pick the skill.

7. Pick it randomly as a fun activity: pull it out of a hat or print the skills individually and plant them around the house, choosing first one your child encounters, etc.

Once you have picked the skill, here are some general ideas for working with your child.

1. Unless it would make him or her oppositional, show lots of enthusiasm for the endeavor: talk about it, make visuals, involve family and friends—celebrate it.

2. Model the skill and point out when you are modeling it. For example:
   • "Didn't I show good tact just now?"

- "Dad's feeling very happy, at a 'four,' because I said I would make pizza for dinner!"
- "What did you think of the way I used positive words with that man, did you notice it? I could tell he really appreciated it."
- "Everyone else wants to go see the other movie—I will just be flexible here and go along with that."
- "I see some people coming toward us, I'm going to make sure I smile and look at them and have a friendly face, it's the nice thing to do."
- "Your baby sister was crying when she woke up, but I used super positive body language and voice tone when I talked to her and she is all happy now!"

3. Set a regular time to review and talk about the skills and tools. It could be at bedtime for fifteen minutes, every Sunday morning before everyone else wakes up, or in the car while you are waiting for his brother to finish soccer practice. While watching TV, check out the body language while you watch it together and discuss it. What is that person feeling? What do they really mean? How can you tell?

4. Make it fun and do it with humor. If your child appreciates humor and "craziness," make it fun and crazy! Here are some fun ideas:
   - Pull the next skill and/or element you are going to work on out of a hat weekly.
   - Stick reminders in strange places that he will find.
   - Use painter's tape or masking tape to put a continuum line on the floor and ask friends/family to stand where they think they are for preferences/opinions.
   - Do another tape line on the floor with an arrow from "weaker" to "stronger" and have friends and family find their spots there for a variety of skills (maybe re-do the "find your spot" game weekly on the target skill to see if anyone thinks they have improved).
   - Set a timer to see how many comfortable or uncomfortable feeling words he can come up with in one minute. This can be extended to other timed activities such as making a positive word choice to each person in the house in the next five minutes, writing down one good thing about having ASD in the next two minutes, or showing positive listening body language while his little sister reads to him for five minutes.
   - Do "copy me and blend" games—can he do what you are doing and look natural?

5. Make your child the Problem-Solver-In-Chief at home. Bring him in on the personal dynamics in your home and give him responsibilities for helping to figure out what the issues are, the perspectives of others, and what a fair solution would be.

Regarding specific skill elements, we recommend trying these ideas for the following.

1. Increasing the frequency of the skill
   - Cue it: make visual cues (words or pictures that you post somewhere) or post and use an appropriate tool for it (blank tools can be found at the end of Chapter Three).
   - Model it: you and family members all do it.
   - Notice it: mark it on a chart or calendar, give him a big gold star every day/week/month he does it, tie a ribbon in her room to mark that you saw her do it, etc.

- Make it a game or competition: this might work well for siblings, cousins, or friends. Positive word choices, voice tone, listening body language, or demonstrating acceptance could work well in the home for competition.
- Make it happen over and over: set it up so that he must practice the skill. For example, during a week of positively expressing the strengths and weaknesses of others, have him tell you one good thing about a person that he knows. Look ahead on your calendar for teachable moments; birthdays and Christmas are great times to practice tact. Make sure he or she is prepared to receive unwanted presents tactfully by practicing tactful responses to the giver.
- Rewards: set up a reward system for showing progress (if he does X, he gets Y).

2. Increasing the situations/places he exhibits the skill
   - Have a visual cue that you carry with you and set up in any place you go. This could be a gesture from you that you both agree on, but an object or icon of some kind that you quickly show to him or that he carries has more potential for independence down the road for him to cue himself with.
   - Pick a room or a circumstance he will exhibit the skill in and give reminders when you are in that room or circumstance, or set up a visual cue there. This could be anything from a stuffed animal to turning a lamp around. When he hears or sees the cue, he knows he is responsible for doing the target skill element.
   - Select a single visual cue in the house that you agree upon and move it from room to room. This could be fun and surprising for your child to see where it turns up! When he sees it, he knows he is responsible for doing the target skill element.

3. Increasing the people the skill occurs with
   - Designate a "target person" he must always do the skill with, add more people over time. Make it visual by putting a sticker or another agreed-upon mark on them.
   - When you're with a group of people, see how many people he can do the skill with (if that is appropriate). For example, using a positive voice tone, acknowledging others, responding verbally to others, blending, or showing appropriate body language at a party. Pick one and start counting!

4. Increasing independence in doing the skill
   - Encourage and/or reward your child to self-report on doing the skill when you are not around to see it. Have a chart or some other way to mark that it was done.
   - Make a visual or designate a visual cue, whether it be a cell phone, a coin, a polished stone, etc., that can be carried and will remind him/her to do a certain skill.
   - Get her to accept responsibility for doing a skill on her own and celebrate success!
   - Ask family members to model the target skill. Ask him to look for it and when he sees them doing it he can pass out small rewards or acknowledgements.

FINAL THOUGHTS

By developing your child's social-communication skills as presented in this book, you are creating the foundation for the soft skills that are most likely to increase his or her vocational success (as discussed in

Chapter Two). Vocational success translates to independence and very possibly peer relationships, so it is very important to your child's future. Through your efforts and with the guidance of this book, after he or she completes his or her academic education we hope that your child is not only employable but also can become employed at a level that is satisfying and optimizes his or her "hard skills," cognitive abilities, and income potential. Your child is only in school for a handful of years with a long adulthood to follow. Although it is easy to become focused on school and the issues therein while he is young, we urge you to keep in mind the long-term priority of *employability* and recognize that it is not the same as academic or cognitive potential, and may not be much influenced by either one in the end. By introducing the foundational social-communication skills concepts and associated tools to support the soft skills needed from a young age and making them a part of your lives over the course of years, you are likely to increase his or her success in adulthood.

In this chapter we have been discussing extending foundational skills with more elements, increased appropriateness and independence, and more functionality. You might have noticed that in giving ideas about how to extend those skills and increase the elements of them, we sometimes described creating opportunities for your child to fail, to have disappointment, or to be uncomfortable. In order to practice these skills, she will need to be challenged in ways that are probably not comfortable for either you or your child. Many children with ASD have "triggers," or issues that elicit a strong negative response from them. A trigger might be a word that she doesn't like to hear, smells, sights, sounds, people, places, or circumstances such as failing, dealing with misunderstandings, being kept apart from a strong interest, and so forth. He or she may get upset talking about ASD, especially initially. At certain times in your life and in your child's life, avoiding triggers may be practical and positive. However, with a view toward developing fully the soft skills for employability, we urge you to consciously and systematically take on triggers using the foundational social-communication skills concepts, activities, suggestions, and tools in this book to help you. It may take considerable time, patience, and hard work, but it will be worth it. Through your efforts and with the guidance of this book, your child can grow up prepared for the challenges of adulthood: employment, relationships, and independence. Good luck!

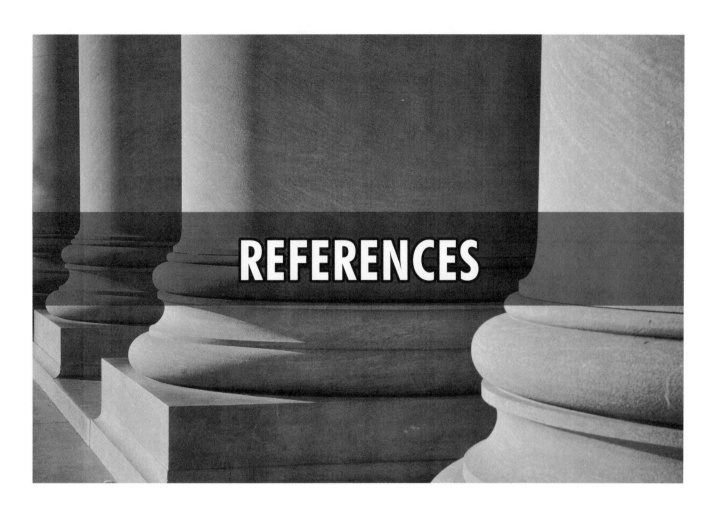

REFERENCES

REFERENCES

CHAPTER ONE

2008. "Easter Seals' Living With Autism Study." Retrieved from http://es.easterseals.com/site/DocServer/Study_FINAL_Harris_12.4.08_Compressed.pdf?docID=83143

"What Is Autism-DSM 5 Diagnostic Criteria." Retrieved from https://www.autismspeaks.org/what-autism/diagnosis/dsm-5-diagnostic-criteria

"Social Communication Disorders in School-Age Children." Retrieved from http://www.asha.org/Practice-Portal/Clinical-Topics/Social-Communication-Disorders-in-School-Age-Children/

Christensen DL, J Baio , KV Braun et al. 2012. "Prevalence and Characteristics of Autism Spectrum Disorder Among Children Aged 8 Years — Autism and Developmental Disabilities Monitoring Network." 11 Sites, United States. MMWR Surveill Summ 2016;65(No. SS-3)(No. SS-3):1–23. DOI: http://dx.doi.org/10.15585/mmwr.ss6503a1.

2012. "Autism Speaks Family Services Employment Think Tank." Retrieved from https://www.autismspeaks.org/sites/default/files/as_think_tank_exec_summary_web1.pdf

Lippman, L. H., R. Ryberg, R. Carney, and K.A. Moore. 2015. "Key 'Soft Skills' That Foster Youth Workforce Success: Toward a Consensus Across Fields." Retrieved from https://www.childtrends.org/wp-content/uploads/2015/06/2015-24AWFCSoftSkillsExecSum.pdf

2015. "Top 10 Soft Skills Employers Want and Why You Need Them." Retrieved from https://www.vc.edu/vc-news/2015-12/top-10-soft-skills-employers-want-and-why-you-need-them/

Brathwaite, S. 2017. "4 Soft Skills Every Tech Professional Should Have." Retrieved from http://www.businessnewsdaily.com/7860-skills-employers-want.html

2015. "The Hard Time Employers Have Finding Soft Skills." Retrieved from http://burning-glass.com/wp-content/uploads/Human_Factor_Baseline_Skills_FINAL.pdf

Doyle, A. (2017, June 21). Top 7 Most Important Soft Skills. Retrieved from https://www.thebalance.com/top-soft-skills-2063721

"Soft Skills to Pay the Bills — Mastering Soft Skills for Workplace Success." Retrieved from https://www.dol.gov/odep/topics/youth/softskills/

2013. "State of St. Louis Workforce 2013." Retrieved from http://www.stlcc.edu/Workforce-Solutions/St-Louis-Workforce/Reports/State-of-St-Louis-Workforce-Report-2013.pdf

Heckman, J. and T. Kautz. 2012. "Hard Evidence on Soft Skills." Retrieved from http://www.nber.org/papers/w18121.pdf

Roux, A.M., P.T. Shattuck, B.P. Cooper, K.A. Anderson, M. Wagner, and S.C. Narendorf. 2013. "Postsecondary employment experiences among young adults with an autism spectrum disorder." *Journal of the American Academy of Child and Adolescent Psychiatry*, 52(9): 931-939.

"IDEA Sec. 300.43 Transition services." Retrieved from https://sites.ed.gov/idea/regs/b/a/300.43

CHAPTER TWO

Heckman, J. and T. Kautz. 2012. "Hard Evidence on Soft Skills." Retrieved from http://www.nber.org/papers/w18121.pdf

2015. "Top 10 Soft Skills Employers Want and Why You Need Them." Retrieved from https://www.vc.edu/vc-news/2015-12/top-10-soft-skills-employers-want-and-why-you-need-them/

2015. "The Hard Time Employers Have Finding Soft Skills." Retrieved from http://burning-glass.com/wp-content/uploads/Human_Factor_Baseline_Skills_FINAL.pdf

Buhl, L. (n.d.). "6 soft skills everyone needs and employers look for." Retrieved from https://www.monster.com/career-advice/article/six-soft-skills-everyone-needs-hot-jobs

Lippman, L. H., R. Ryberg, R. Carney, and K.A. Moore. 2015. "Key 'Soft Skills' That Foster Youth Workforce Success: Toward a Consensus Across Fields." Retrieved from https://www.childtrends.org/wp-content/uploads/2015/06/2015-24AWFCSoftSkillsExecSum.pdf

Astington, J., and M. Edward. 2010. "The Development of Theory of Mind in Early Childhood." Retrieved from http://www.child-encyclopedia.com/sites/default/files/textes-experts/en/588/the-development-of-theory-of-mind-in-early-childhood.pdf

Edelson, S. (n.d.). "Theory of Mind." Retrieved from https://www.autism.com/understanding_theoryofmind

"Social Communication Disorders in School-Age Children." Retrieved from http://www.asha.org/Practice-Portal/Clinical-Topics/Social-Communication-Disorders-in-School-Age-Children/

ABOUT THE AUTHORS

DIANE ZAJAC earned a master's degree in social work and a bachelor's degree in psychology from Wayne State University. She has worked twenty years in elementary and middle school settings, supporting the social communication needs of hundreds of students on the autism spectrum. She also works to improve the employability skills of young adults with ASD as a job coach in the community.

LISA TEW graduated from Purdue University with a master's degree in speech and language pathology. Lisa has worked to improve communication and related functional skills of hundreds of children and young adults on the autism spectrum, in a variety of settings, for over thirty years. Lisa currently works with middle and high school students, many of whom have autism spectrum disorder. She is also a transition coordinator in the schools, helping students with disabilities to make positive post-secondary transitions to independence, higher education, and/or employment.

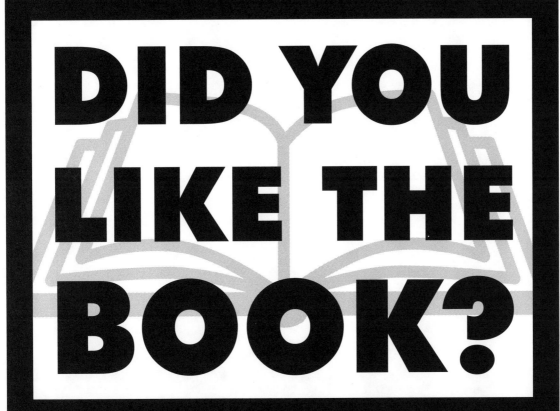

More books for older teens on the autism spectrum!

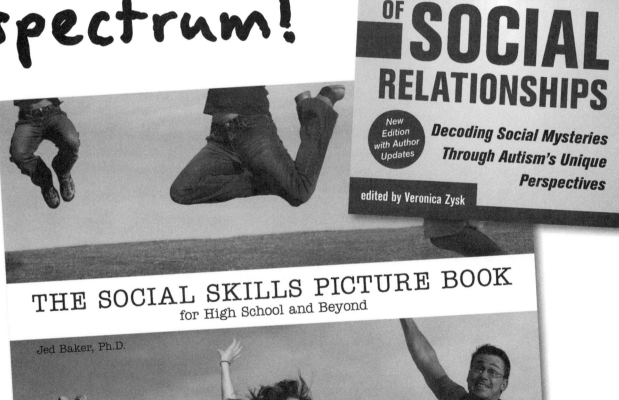

UNWRITTEN RULES

Dr. Temple Grandin & Sean Barron

OF SOCIAL RELATIONSHIPS

New Edition with Author Updates

Decoding Social Mysteries Through Autism's Unique Perspectives

edited by Veronica Zysk

THE SOCIAL SKILLS PICTURE BOOK
for High School and Beyond

Jed Baker, Ph.D.

800•489•0727 | www.FHautism.com

FUTURE HORIZONS INC.

You Can Take It With You!